POPE FRANCIS AND THE THEOLOGY OF THE PEOPLE

Rafael Luciani

Translated by Phillip Berryman

ORBIS BOOKS

Maryknoll, New York 10545

ORBIS BOOKS
Maryknoll, New York 10545

Fathers and Brothers
MARYKNOLL

Founded in 1970, Orbis Books endeavors to publish works that enlighten the mind, nourish the spirit, and challenge the conscience. The publishing arm of the Maryknoll Fathers and Brothers, Orbis seeks to explore the global dimensions of the Christian faith and mission, to invite dialogue with diverse cultures and religious traditions, and to serve the cause of reconciliation and peace. The books published reflect the views of their authors and do not represent the official position of the Maryknoll Society. To learn more about Maryknoll and Orbis Books, please visit our website at www.mary-knollsociety.org.

Library of Congress Cataloging-in-Publication Data

Names: Luciani, Rafael, author.
Title: Pope Francis and the theology of the people / Rafael Luciani ;
    translated by Phillip Berryman.
Other titles: Papa Francisco y la teolog?ia del pueblo. English
Description: Maryknoll : Orbis Books, 2017. | Includes bibliographical
    references and index.
Identifiers: LCCN 2017011699 (print) | LCCN 2017027166 (ebook) | ISBN
    9781608337170 (e-book) | ISBN 9781626982529 (pbk.)
Subjects: LCSH: Francis, Pope, 1936– | Liberation theology. | Catholic
    Church—Doctrines.
Classification: LCC BX1378.7 (ebook) | LCC BX1378.7 .L8313 2017 (print) | DDC
    230/.2092—dc23
LC record available at https://lccn.loc.gov/2017011699

POPE FRANCIS
AND THE THEOLOGY
OF THE PEOPLE

Contents

Foreword

On March 13, 2013, when it was announced on the balcony over St. Peter's Square that the new pope was calling himself Francis and that he had come from the ends of the earth, the Church knew that it was entering a new era. It knew so only intuitively because not much can be known about a person in five minutes. In those first minutes he simply looked over the crowd with both surprise and emotion, greeted it with a friendly "Good evening," and humbly asked for a blessing. That was enough. The intuition of the world, united actually and virtually in the square, recognized that we were facing a different pope, someone who in his first gestures brought a freshness for which many yearned, while believing it unattainable.

In his first actions, the pope reaffirmed from that balcony the intuition of that Roman evening. He traveled on the same bus as the other cardinals; he went in person to pay the bill for his stay at the clergy guesthouse; and, like any parish priest with the least bit of pastoral sensitivity, he went to greet his parishioners at the church door at the end of the Mass. Many of us were happy, and we felt that this closeness did not in the least undermine his status as bishop of Rome and head of the Catholic Church, *primus inter pares.*

But the freshness did not merely consist of gestures devoid of content. Little by little it became known that behind Francis was a theology with a regional flavor, prepared in the crucible of thought that dared to recognize a place for popular religiosity as an integral part of religious virtue and for popular culture as a specific and meaningful way of living the faith. One of the main currents of theological insight in Argentina was conceived in proximity to the very poor and involved directing the Church's efforts at evangelization outward toward the vast majority excluded from church structures. Today we are familiar with this theological current under the name "theology of the people." Lucio Gera, Rafael Tello, and Juan Carlos Scannone are the figures commonly mentioned as most involved in shaping this thought, although they are surely not the only ones. Cardinal Bergoglio knew these men and their thought; he made their theological conclusions his own in his pastoral work when he was archbishop of Buenos Aires, and he has reaffirmed those conclusions in his papal ministry.

Rafael Luciani proposes to take us back to the springs from which Francis drank so that we may better understand the chief characteristics of his is papacy. He correctly sets Francis's actions not only in the Argentine context but also in the context of Latin American thought, closely connected to options for liberation in a variety of situations. It is important to note the relationship between liberation theology and the theology of the people, and to emphasize that their nuances converge in complementarity and not in confrontation. That Luciani grasps this connection is evident from his words at the very beginning of this book, where he notes that in the theology of the people, "the option is for the poor, from the life-world of the poor, respecting their own way of being in order to recognize them, affectively and effectively, as true agents of a historical process of development and liberation." Thus, he returns to the proposal of a liberation that can be considered from different angles, but that seeks a single non-negotiable aim.

Nevertheless, the author does not simply offer a historical presentation on the roots of Francis's thought. Instead, he addresses the main lines of what he calls Francis's "pastoral geopolitics." The pope's teaching contains an invitation to enter into realities in church and society not just superficially but in depth, fostering a change of cultural paradigm that may allow us to renew a personal encounter with Jesus Christ and with our neighbor, especially with the poorest. Thus, Luciani can clearly maintain that, based on our pope's reflection and action, "healing the age means, more than ever, reconnecting with the life-world of the poor, the despised and excluded, those for whom there is no room in society, those who have no future, in other words, all those who are outside any system, *with no possibility of having possibilities*, from the economic and political to the religious and ecclesial realm. It is here that the need is posed today to rethink the option for the poor in terms of the defense of the peoples and their cultures, in terms of sociocultural realities, and to set out on a journey of response to the new signs of the times of our age."

It is always good to have in hand a book that helps us learn the origins of a body of thought, and which, at the same time, impels us toward the transformation of a future of which we are real agents. I think Rafael Luciani's book meets both of these conditions: we have here a contribution that helps clarify a theological and pastoral understanding that originated and has developed under the skies of Argentina,

but which from the outset has been open to the cultural newness furnished to us by all of Latin America. This body of
thought is very rich but still unfamiliar to many in its nuances
and varied dimensions. Someone who undertakes the effort
to explain it deserves our gratitude.

Rev. Dr. Omar César Albado
Faculty of Theology
Catholic University of Argentina

The Primacy of the Christian

God, in Christ,
redeems not only the individual person,
but also the social relations existing between people.
(*Evangelii Gaudium* 178)

A theological-pastoral option

Pope Francis's apostolic journey to South America in July 2015 through Ecuador, Bolivia, and Paraguay represented an important turning point for understanding his papacy. It was the beginning of a stage in which he would make clear the connection between his speeches and the theological and pastoral guidelines proposed by what is known as the theology of the people, or the theology of culture. That connection had first been introduced in 2013 with the publication of the apostolic exhortation *Evangelii Gaudium* (*EG*).

Francis's thought and actions are grounded in a theological and pastoral approach that guides his roadmap for the church today. The theological dimension of this approach was initially nourished by the theology of the people, one of the various branches of liberation theology that developed in Latin American. The origin of the pastoral dimension can be found in the process of renewal that was driven by the type of ministry proposed by the Argentine bishops at San Miguel (1969) in adapting the conclusions of the Second General Conference of Latin American Bishops, or CELAM (CELAM II, Medellín, 1968) to their local situation. Both are instances of clearly implementing the spirit of Vatican II, an effort that over the years would be deepened at the Third General Conference of Latin American Bishops (CELAM III, Puebla, 1979) and would eventually lead to the generation of a critically important statement, the concluding document of the Fifth General Conference of the Bishops of Latin America and the Caribbean (CELAM V, Aparecida, 2007).

At the Aparecida assembly, the then cardinal Bergoglio was named president of the commission that was charged with drafting the concluding document. This work was to shape his entire papacy, so much so that Francis sometimes gives a copy of the *Aparecida Document* to the heads of state and church representatives whom he receives in the Vatican or meets during his apostolic journeys. Indeed, *Aparecida* speaks to the radical change taking place in the era in which we are living, and to the Church's need to be reformed in order to be able to respond to the new signs of the times, especially the situation of poor people. This is what he said to his priests in Buenos Aires while reflecting on Aparecida:

> At Aparecida the Church becomes aware of what has been noted for a number of years. What we are experiencing is a "change of era"; what is happening is that the very framework is changing. The changes have to do not with "the multiple partial meanings that individuals can find in the everyday actions that they perform, but [with] the meaning that gives unity to

everything that exists" (*Aparecida* 37). What is specific
to the "change of era" is that things are no longer in
their place. What previously served for explaining the
world, relationships, good and evil, doesn't seem to
work anymore. How we are situated in history has
changed. Things that we never thought would happen, or at least that we weren't going to see, we're
seeing them and we don't even dare to think about
the future.[1]

The vision of Francis cannot be disconnected from the
great theological debates over culture and evangelization in
the Latin American Church. That is why we can highlight the
influence that certain Argentine theologians, such as Lucio
Gera and Rafael Tello, have had on him. They have helped
him to understand that pastoral activity and theology should
form a unity centered on awareness of the culture of poor, ordinary people and their religion, their needs, their future,
their concerns and hopes, and that this cannot take place apart
from the struggle for the liberation of peoples within the
framework of respect for the preservation of their sociocultural milieu. Thus, Francis takes the path indicated by Vatican
II in *Gaudium et Spes* (*GS*). In addition, drawing on the
Uruguayan thinker Alberto Methol Ferré, he delves deeper
into the way this "change of era" confronts the Church with
a new challenge: that of responding pastorally and geopolitically to the dominant tendency of cultural globalization,
which is a form of leveling that does away with local cultures.
Facing this reality of our age, the Church must go out of itself to meet people and their cultures. Only thus can it be
faithful to its mission as people of God dwelling in the midst
of the peoples of the earth.

Gospel hermeneutics of cultures

Many who are not familiar with the specific framework of this theological and pastoral perspective have proposed unconvincing models for interpreting the roadmap of Francis's papacy. For example, there has been a tendency to assess his work on the basis of a mere pastoral *aggiornamento* of the Church, an approach inspired by the principles of the Church's social doctrine while also highlighting more radical aspects having to do with the discernment of contemporary economic and political models. Others have assessed him as one who is promoting a process of renewal of ecclesial culture through reforms that will change the way the church institution operates, whether as the result of radical Christian thought or of making continuing decisions based on radical realism. Such modes of interpretation take their bearings from sociocultural paradigms and criteria of discernment foreign to the hermeneutics of the culture of ordinary people followed by Francis. It is not surprising that some analysts, unable to comprehend the world of specific meanings that inspire his vision of society, the Church, and God, portray the pope as a populist or demagogue.

Although the pope makes use of the Church's social teaching, as did his predecessors, this cannot be confused with the broader horizon of meaning present in his theological and pastoral approach, which was formed within the context of popular movements, ecclesial communities, and theological-pastoral debates regarding reception of the teachings of Vatican II in Latin America. Accordingly, Francis does not carry out his discernment by focusing simply on papal authority with regard to the social doctrine of the Church, which offers principles and criteria for judgment of sociopolitical and economic situations[2] while neglecting to propose concrete sociopolitical mediations for the liberation of peoples.[3]

Instead, Francis proposes a gospel hermeneutic of culture in a prophetic—rather than a doctrinal or a cultic—key, and takes the praxis of Jesus as the primary reference point for all theologico-pastoral activity aimed at generating processes of change in today's global mindset. That is what he says in *Evangelii Gaudium*: "What I would like to propose is something much more in the line of an evangelical discernment. It is the approach of a missionary disciple" (*EG* 50). Thus, for him there is no magisterium that is not social, because the kerygma itself is "inescapably social" (*EG* 177); what Jesus proposes in preaching the Kingdom of God is a new design for society, one of life in kinship (*EG* 180–181).

We can say that the pope engages in ongoing discernment of the sociocultural, economic, and ecclesial realms, to mention just three that have a global impact. In the sociocultural realm, our globalized world tends to render us incapable as agents; that is, it relativizes the absolute value of people and their cultures and thus suppresses the diversity that gives human relevance and meaning to everyday life. New subcultures of indolence arise, fostering dehumanization to the point of rejection of anyone who is not in tune with the dominant system and its pursuit of monetary gain.

Thus it is that in the economic realm Francis questions systems and policies that absolutize finance, placing its value above that of human persons and their full development and willing to discard the majority of humankind, the poor, regarding them as mere objects destined to live *with no possibility of having possibilities*. Meanwhile, this is happening in an era that has achieved an accumulation of wealth and a level of technical development that allows for the elimination of poverty. And yet, paradoxically, it is an era marked by the greatest socioeconomic inequality in history.

Finally, in the religious realm, the pope's voice is raised against an ecclesial culture that has taken root in the institutional church, a warped pathology of clerical power. Such an ecclesial culture calls into question its fidelity to the Gospel as well as the credibility of the Catholic Church today. We must honestly ask whether we are living non-Christian forms of Catholicism—in other words, a Christianity without Jesus, devoid of the Gospel. Hence the need for a church that goes out, in the manner of Jesus, to look at matters from the peripheries, a church that makes an option for the poor and against their poverty. Such a church is not self-referential; it understands itself as a servant of humankind rather than as a power wielding authority over personal consciences and public spaces.

These realms—sociocultural, economic, and ecclesial—are undergoing a systemic crisis that has to do not simply with whether their organization and administrative functioning is valid, but with the collapse of the paradigms of society and religion on which they are based. Specifically, in the West, there is a structural crisis in the way in which Christianity is being transmitted, a crisis that often goes unrecognized even by the ecclesiastical institution. It is an open question whether the ecclesiastical institution, in its present hierarchical and organizational arrangement is open to taking on the consequences of the Second Vatican Council's spirit, or whether it is still engaged—as it appears to be—in resisting, opposing, or simply being indifferent to the signs of the times that Francis has identified. This entire situation points toward the need for a conversion, a change of mindset.

A mindset to be overcome

The actions of Francis have been aimed at desacralizing an institution which, since the time of Constantine, has presented itself as sacred and untouchable. Indeed, in line with the spirit of the council, the pope is responding to the signs of the times with creative fidelity, trying to do what Jesus would do today.[4] Francis says so himself:

> Vatican II was a re-reading of the Gospel in light of contemporary culture. It produced a renewal movement that simply comes from the Gospel itself. Its fruits are enormous. Just recall the liturgy. The work of liturgical reform has been a service to the people as a re-reading of the Gospel from a concrete historical situation. Yes, there are hermeneutics of continuity and discontinuity, but one thing is clear: the dynamic of reading the Gospel, actualizing its message for today—which was typical of Vatican II—is absolutely irreversible.[5]

This poses a serious challenge to the church institution today. It calls for revision of a mindset centered on worship and church buildings. As then archbishop Bergoglio observed in his first meeting with the Priests' Council of Buenos Aires in 2008:

> What seemed normal to us in the family, the church, society, and the world, is not likely to return to being that way. What we are experiencing isn't something that we have to endure, deludedly waiting for things to go back to being as they always

were … "The pastoral conversion of our communities requires moving from a pastoral ministry of mere conservation to a decidedly missionary pastoral ministry … making the Church visibly present as a mother who reaches out, a welcoming home, a constant school of missionary communion" (*Aparecida* 370).

With the bishops at Aparecida, Francis understands that in the current situation to speak of personal conversion is not enough; we must extend our efforts to the reform of structures and to changes in the styles of church life. Only thus can the Church be a sign of credibility for global society. "Pastoral conversion is experienced when 'social and cultural transformations naturally represent new challenges to the Church in its mission of building the Kingdom of God. Hence the need, in fidelity to the Holy Spirit who leads it, for an ecclesial renewal that entails spiritual, pastoral, and also institutional reforms' (*Aparecida* 367)."[6]

The path of reform spoken of by Bergoglio at Aparecida in 2007 would be the one put forth by Francis in *Evangelii Gaudium* in 2013. It is not, however, a path of regression to the past, to the old structures for preserving religion and ecclesial culture, but rather a path forward, toward a process of radical change in mindsets and structures—because "our faithful people want pastors of people and not state clerics, functionaries."[7]

A primacy to be recognized

How are we to understand this process of change? What is the starting point? For Francis it is not a matter of simply reforming discipline and the forms of church life, thus merely reshuffling organizational and administrative procedures. That was the kind of reform carried out at the Council of Trent, where everything was prescribed and severe penalties were spelled out, where the law was absolutized and set above the spirit and concrete pastoral discernment. For Francis, true reform begins with changing the ecclesial mindset, which means giving primacy to the spirit over the law.

Francis clearly describes this primacy of the spirit in his address to the pontifical universities:

> Research and study ought to be integrated with personal and community life, with missionary commitment, with fraternal charity and sharing with the poor, with care of the interior life in relationship with the Lord. Your institutes are not machines for producing theologians and philosophers; they are communities in which one grows, and that growing occurs in the family. In the university family there is the charism of governance, entrusted to the superiors, and there is the diaconate of the non-teaching staff, which is indispensable for creating a family atmosphere in everyday life and also for creating the attitude of humanity and of practical wisdom that will make the students of today people capable of building humanity, of transmitting the truth in a human dimension, of understanding that if one lacks the goodness and the beauty of belonging to a workaday family one ends up being an intellectual without talent, an ethicist without goodness, a thinker lacking in a sense of the splendor of beauty and masked in formalisms. The daily, respectful contact with hard work and the witness of the men and

women who work in your institutions will give you
that dose of realism that is so necessary to ensure that
your knowledge will be human and not that of the
laboratory.[8]

Recovering the primacy of what is truly Christian means
going to the essentials of the "new and living way opened" by
Jesus (Heb 10:20). Or, as Francis puts it, of "living human life
to the fullest" (*EG* 75) and allowing this to permeate "work
and production, human settlements, ways of life, language
and artistic expression, political organization, and everyday
life."[9] This is the way to build "closeness" and to "free ourselves from the captivity expressed in the dynamic of exclusion, through attitudes such as indifference, intolerance,
extreme individualism, and sectarianism."[10] "Otherwise, reality is fragmented."[11]

For Francis, the consequences of returning to the council's spirit necessarily involve rethinking our model of religion. Within the Latin American Church and its theological
community there has been ongoing debate regarding this for
years, and it has now become particularly relevant under the
current papacy. The Venezuelan theologian Pedro Trigo, SJ,
offers the following thoughts:

Assimilation [of the teachings] of Vatican II at Medellín entailed in principle reestablishing the primacy of
the Christian, something that was being practiced to
an extraordinary degree in grassroots communities
and groups in solidarity with them. There the Mass
was again the Lord's Supper of the communities of
the early centuries. Faith, hope, and charity were embodied in life and were celebrated with great joy and
creativity in the Lord's Supper. However, since the

central initiatives of Vatican II were not accepted, there has been strong pressure to return to the neolithic triad, which relegates Christians to being the objects of cultic action performed by priests. Since the beginning of this century it has become clear in our region that the environment is no longer permeated by Christianity and no longer transmits it. In the light of this realization, which many find worrisome, a considerable portion of the church institution barricades itself in what it regards as the absolute minimum that must be defended, which in practice for those involved is not the Gospel, but the triad of church buildings, priests, and sacrifices: neolithic religion. Ultimately, they are defending themselves, identified with their borders.[12]

Is it possible to change paradigms[13] and to leave behind a model of Christianity that abides within the parameters of a neolithic private religion? Only if we live out our humanity with the same intensity as Jesus. As Aparecida reminded us: "We must all start again from Christ, recognizing that being Christian is not the result of an ethical choice or a lofty idea, but an encounter with an event, a person, which gives life a new horizon and a decisive direction" (*Aparecida* 12).

THEOLOGY AND THE PEOPLE: *SENSUS POPULI*

Always remember the poor (Gal 2:10)

In the context of a theology of the people of God

In 1966, in response to the new atmosphere brought about by Vatican II, the Argentine Bishops Conference formed the Bishops Pastoral Commission, known as COEPAL.[1] Its aim was to internalize the spirit of the council and to propose a national pastoral plan. Initially the commission was comprised of Bishops Enrique Angelelli, Vicente Zazpe, and Manuel Marengo. Also in the group were two Argentine experts who would attend CELAM II in Medellín: Father Lucio Gera and the Jesuit Alberto Sily.[2] It was in Argentina that what was to be known as the "theology of the people" first began to take shape, taking on the task of developing a communal form of being church within a collegial structure. The church in Argentina discerned the change of era in the following terms:

> Our great task at this time, in order to bring about the post-council stage, must consist of three things:

(1) Being imbued by the council; assimilating it by reflecting and internalizing its ideas and its spirit; (2) Consolidating and improving the communal form of the Church and its collegial structures: assembly of bishops, presbyterate, pastoral council, structuring and coordination of the laity; (3) Fostering greater openness to the world on the part of clergy and laity. This entails greater sincerity in fostering the spirit of poverty and service. In order to carry out this program, the Church in Argentina must increase reflection and dialogue in all sectors and on all levels.[3]

The document sought to express a vision of Church that would respond to the council spirit, especially the demands posed in *Gaudium et Spes* for situating the Church in the contemporary world. It was understood that the Church's action ought to give primacy to human relations in terms of salvation history as opposed to simply fostering a sense of institutional belonging. This primacy was inspired by what the bishops at the 1968 meeting in Medellín would describe as the just "aspiration to liberation and growth in humanity"[4] of every human being. Following the spirit of *aggiornamento*, the Argentine bishops committed themselves to carrying out a reform of mindset and of the norms governing church structures. They desired that the Church attain a "clearer awareness of itself, reform, dialogue with other Christian brothers and sisters, and openness to the world of today: the four aims of the council."[5]

The consequences for the life of faith were clear. Pastoral action and theological reflection were needed in order to respond to this "new age in human history"[6] as the council had defined it. It was an era that was witnessing "the birth of a new humanism, where people are defined first of all by their responsibility to their brothers and sisters and to history."[7] This new awareness regarded it as the proper task of the Christian to "work with everyone in building a more human world."[8] It meant taking a stand toward reality in which religion could not be understood without social commitment, where salvation and the effort toward transforming history were intertwined. This is what was very clearly stated by the Argentine bishops in 1966:

> We regret the pernicious influence of those who accuse religion of being opposed to human liberation, and we reject the charge that hope in another life lessens interest in temporal tasks. On the contrary, we claim that recognizing God increases in us Christians a sense of human dignity.[9]

Basically, this meant assuming and putting into practice the ecclesiology of the people of God proposed by *Lumen Gentium* (*LG*). Lucio Gera speaks of this in two passages that we regard as significant, in which he describes the Church as people of God in the midst of the peoples of the earth:

> God in his mystery has set out to "make people holy and save them not as individuals, without bond or link between one another, [but] to bring them together as one people " (*Lumen Gentium* 9). God does not simply call individuals, but invites them; thus in calling them, he brings them together with others. God—in Christ—invites believers to bring them together on another, more profound level of human intercommunion and shared life.
>   While indeed the people of God transcends any people, it is called to be incarnated in all the peoples

of the earth. "The one people of God is present in all the peoples of the earth, because it takes its citizens from all nations...The people of God...is made up of different peoples " (*Lumen Gentium* 13).[10]

This reading of *Gaudium et Spes* and *Lumen Gentium* together made it possible to move beyond the vision of a private and insignificant religion, one with no connection to reality and nourished solely by its liturgical expression. The reading makes clear that being Christian entails daily interpersonal relationships. It is here that the expression "people of God" becomes meaningful and takes on life, because "the one people of God is present in all the peoples of the earth."[11] Here we can see how ecclesiological reception of Vatican II in Argentina was a first step toward the development of a theology of the people, as explained in the words of Gera:

> The Church takes place as intercommunion between human beings—not only as relationship of humans with God, but as interrelationship of human beings among themselves. The relationship with the other is not simply something added to a Church already constituted by a relationship with God. The relationship with the other is also constitutive of the Church, that is, it is set within the very essence of being Church.[12]

Francis would articulate this ecclesiological insight as an inclusive, relational soteriology in continuity with *Lumen Gentium*. He believes that "being Church is being people of God,"[13] that we are not saved alone but in relationship—in what we are and live with others—and that God is revealed in the warp and woof of the history of the people.[14] This is the vision that would be expressed in *Evangelii Gaudium*: "God has chosen to call them together as a people and not as isolated individuals. No one is saved by himself or herself, individually, or by his or her own efforts. God attracts us by taking into account the complex interweaving of personal relationships entailed in the life of a human community. This people which God has chosen and called is the Church."[15] That is, it is impossible to be Church as people of God without recognition and action *within*—not above or out in front of—the peoples of this world.

It was Lucio Gera who, over the course of the process of reflection and discussion, gave this particular way of doing Latin American theology its own proper profile. In his view, the theology of the people did not seek to change social and political structures in themselves, but to promote a discernment of the mission and identity of the ecclesiastical institution based on an explicit option for poor people and their culture. And, as Rafael Tello adds, the notion of people is connected to that of the existence of a popular culture, because, "if a people lasts for centuries, the popular culture that characterizes it has to last for the same period of time. Therefore, in order to understand a people for who they really are, they must be seen in terms of what is coextensive with them."[16] That is, one cannot understand a people without taking into account their popular culture as a culture of its own, distinct from modern enlightenment culture. It is impossible to be Church without being incarnate in the midst of the peoples, responding to their cultures. It is out of this ecclesiological option with sociocultural roots that a religious discourse is built, a discourse that drives sociopolitical dialogue and promotes a pastoral praxis informed by social justice as a value of this people that is faithful to Jesus.[17]

Reading Medellín from the perspective of the people

Although COEPAL ended in 1973, many of the theologians belonging to it continued to gather under the intellectual leadership of Lucio Gera.[18] COEPAL's greatest contribution took place in 1969 with the drafting of chapter 6 of the *San Miguel Document*, which dealt with pastoral ministry as the embodiment of a church that wanted to become *people of God in the midst of poor people.*

Among the many discussions that took place, Rafael Tello proposed the key direction that was to characterize this new theological insight in continuity with Latin American theology as a whole. In his words, it was a matter of "unifying all of Medellín in the language of the people."[19] This meant embracing the ecclesiology of the people of God and the method of the signs of the times and reading them from the perspective of the people in their concrete everyday life and their incarnate religious faith. This focus would frame a new sociocultural type of theological locus, leading to a theology worked out from actual pastoral presence and action. In Rafael Tello's words:

> The Argentine church must see itself and its problems from the standpoint of the people. The people would then be the illuminating and unifying element of the problematic of the Church. That means seeing it not in terms of its internal conflicts, its internal difficulties, or its internal issues but in terms of its insertion, as people of God, in the Argentine people. This would lead to a course of action connected to that insertion, namely, the retrieval of the Christian values that are in the people . . . seeing from the viewpoint of

the people and adopting a people-centered approach to pastoral action.[20]

Based on such an understanding, the Church as people of God must discern its presence and action in terms of peoples and their cultures, their realities, their interests and ways of life, since it is they who are the subjects of history. This is the proper sociocultural locus for discerning the signs of our times, as explained in the *San Miguel Document* itself:

> The Church must discern its liberating or saving action from the perspective of the people and their interests, for inasmuch as the people are the subject and agent of human history, which is intimately linked with salvation history, the signs of the times become present and decipherable in the events proper to the people or that affect them.[21]

If the people are the subject and agent of their own history, the Church is in debt to the people, and not the reverse. In other words, it is the *periphery* that gives meaning to the center and not the other way around; it is *daily and sustained relationship*, lived in faith, that shapes a people and gives them meaning as a people of God, and not their belonging to an official religion. The upshot is an incarnational inversion, by which both theological reflection and pastoral action become oriented "toward the people, and primarily from the people itself." What does this mean? In the words of a powerful passage from the *San Miguel Document*,

> this means: loving the people, becoming attuned to them and comprehending them; trusting in their creative capacity and in their transforming power;

helping them to express themselves and organize
themselves; listening to them, grasping and understanding their sayings and forms of expression even
though they may come from a culture different from
our own; being familiar with their joys and hopes,
anxieties and suffering, needs and values; knowing
what they want and desire from the Church and its
ministers; discerning in all of that what should be
corrected or purified, what is currently the case but
only transitory, what has permanent value and holds
promise for the future; not separating from them, or
getting ahead of their real desires and decisions; not
transferring to them issues, attitudes, norms or values that are foreign or alien to them, especially when
these deprive them of or weaken their reasons for living and reasons for hoping.[22]

The people are not a metaphysical unit, nor are they a
mass or a diffused set of individuals without direction or
project. Neither are they the sum of individuals living in
marginal places peripheral to the city. Their being, their dynamic, their way of living and dealing with conflict unfold in
unique ways, in a non-homogenous and non-predetermined
daily life that is vital and always in process.[23] In other words,
"the people as subject of history is not something already
given, finished, something that becomes present at a particular moment, but rather a process, a reality in motion in which
must be detected—and this is not always easy—yearnings,
tendencies both real and apparent, struggles, and so forth."[24]
This entails "perceiving the movement of the people over
the course of history not as an abstraction but in its community life, which is expressed in taking on the particular values that shape a culture. Popular culture and people make

up an inseparable pair"[25]—their connotations are always plural. Consequently, theology has to be contextualized in peoples and their cultures, never outside them, or it will be insignificant and irrelevant, unable to speak to concrete human subjects who live out their personal history in the midst of their everyday life and, from there, think, pray, and give of themselves in solidarity with others, even from their weakness and frailty.

Option for the poor, option for poor peoples

More than a few voices have been raised questioning the presence of the option for the people in the teaching of Pope Francis; some even regard it as populist. Many of the criticisms have come from highly educated sociocultural contexts, even from persons who, while they are concerned about the situation of the poor today, have never dealt personally with them or shared their lives. As Victor Fernandez explains:

> It used to be said that the theology of the people opts for the ignorant masses, people lacking in culture and critical thinking. What the theology of the people advocates is something very different. It means regarding the poor not merely as the object of liberation or education, but as individuals capable of thinking in their own categories, capable of living the faith legitimately in their own manner, capable of forging paths based on their popular culture. Indeed, the fact that they express themselves or look at life differently does not mean that they do not think or have no culture; it is simply a different culture, one that differs from that of the middle class.[26]

What the magisterium of Francis calls for is that the Church make "an option to safeguard those who are today discarded in the formation of a culture's memory,"[27] that it live a prophetic Christianity capable of discerning the ethical validity and moral truth of the sociocultural locations that still do not find space or narrative in public media. This is where a change of direction needs to occur, both in the political life of a country and in the institutional forms that the Church must take if it is to recover its credibility in today's world. Francis believes that the Church must contribute to the process of change, because, "together with the various sectors of society, it supports those programs that best respond to the dignity of each person and the common good" and, by so doing, can propose "in a clear way the fundamental values of human life in order to transmit convictions that can then find expression in political activity."[28]

The cultural shock that this will produce in both the ecclesiastical institution and educated elite society can be overcome only by a process of pastoral conversion or incarnational reversal. We need to ask ourselves: What is the space in which I move, who are those in my circle of friends, what is the sociocultural place out of which I live and think? If the location of the Church, the Christian community, isn't the location of the people, it can hardly be called the people of God, as intended by the council. It may be an ecclesiastical church institution that has worshipers and faithfully communicates an ecclesial culture, but it will not be in a true sense the people of God, whose members are brothers and sisters one to another. It will be an institution unable to make the leap from *mater convocans* to *fraternitas convocata*. In other words, as Rafael Tello points out:

> The church [as institution] cannot turn toward the poor. Or it can do so from outside, from a stance of

service, whether self-serving or not. It works for the poor, among them and even with some of them. That is, it organizes works for the poor, sometimes it sets up those works among them, and sometimes it incorporates some poor people into some work, at least in spirit, but it isn't from them. It is well intentioned, it may often be very positive, but it doesn't take the specific form of what a Church of the incarnate Word would be. Because its Master, Lord, and Way, turned toward human beings not from outside, but by becoming incarnate...Turning toward specific human beings, Christians from among our people, becoming incarnate among them, means doing it while recognizing their faith with affection—their particular mode of Christian life—and their culture—their particular mode of temporal life...And that is resisted by many who see in that faith a less valuable way, tolerable or permissible, but nothing more. Because if that faith were a genuine vocation [a true way of responding to God], it ought to be cultivated, not changed.[29]

Are we able to accept and recognize the existence of a hermeneutics of the people's expression of Christianity? This isn't the same thing as studying popular religiosity. It entails changing our sociocultural location and mindset, initiating a process of conversion in our way of living and speaking. A genuine personal and emotional conversion to the world of the poor—who constitute the majority of humankind—becomes absolutely necessary if we are to grasp the meaning of Christianity today and to respond to this time in which we are called to live. In being converted to the poor, we will come to value in their true dignity these others whom we previously overlooked or looked down on. This will mean entering into their own *ethos*. Here is Lucio Gera's beautiful explanation of this process vis-à-vis the institutional Church, a process that Francis calls *pastoral conversion*:

> In conversion, things—the world—are reinterpreted, they are re-felt—felt in a new way—they are re-done, somewhat like being recreated in their paschal newness; another starting point is used to reconstruct the meaning of the world...The world in all its expanse is re-lived, not as a mere remembrance, which would be going back to live the old, but as resurrection, which is not to be understood only as living again, but as living anew, not as a new life, but living differently.[30]

Understanding the poor as the people, as the collective subject of a history, means discovering and recognizing that they are bearers of a cultural *ethos* of their own, whose religious soul or heart always wagers on hope, even in the limit-experiences and conditions of material deprivation in which they live.[31] But how are we to comprehend this without placing ourselves in the people's life-world, and how can we get to know their values without dealing with them personally and learning their life stories? The re-categorization of our own notions and interpretations will take place only as the result of a life shared with the life-world of the poor, never outside it. Hence, our option for the poor becomes an ethical choice for the people's culture by our knowing, preserving, and empowering it. This goes far beyond mere knowledge of popular religiosity or people's religion. It entails sharing with hope and charity their everyday way of living the faith in a manner that differs from a privatized form of religion.[32] It also differs from a highly educated, scientific, or technical way of speaking about the people, in which "real persons, common individuals in their personal reality, disappear and are worth nothing, and with them the people itself disappears, for the people only exists and *subsists in the persons who make it up.*"[33]

This is something that Francis understands. Hence, in his teaching the word "people" is not reduced to economic and sociopolitical categories, to be analyzed in the light of the Marxist method. Nor does he limit himself to a mere phenomenological description of popular religious expressions, as many academic theologians tend to do. Rather, influenced by the thought of Rafael Tello, the pope understands that the starting point must be a real and daily connection with the poor, the study of popular culture, and a recognition of its own proper *ethos.* This means, in his view, that turning to the poor is a matter of spirit, which "requires love and closeness to the people, so that not only through scholarly research but also through the innate capacity for affective understanding given by love, it can recognize and discern the proper modalities of the culture of the people."[34] Based on this affective relationship it is then possible to become truly conscious of what *de facto* appears as an obstacle to the full development of the people—socioeconomically, politically, and religiously—and of what is positive that must be safeguarded from any external influence that seeks to brainwash them, indoctrinate them, or make them lose their identity. It is along these lines that Francis believes that only "from the affective connaturality born of love can we appreciate the theological life present in the piety of Christian peoples, especially among the poor."[35]

The option for the poor begins from and unfolds in the life-world of the poor themselves. It involves respecting their way of being in order to recognize them honestly and with feeling as true subjects of a historical process of development and liberation. When we stop seeing them as objects of study and begin treating the poor personally, that is when we begin to be evangelized by them. That is the path of conversion, not mediated by the liturgy but by everyday dealing with persons and their life stories. It is in this *shared everyday life* where the beauty of a humanity that has been touched by the divine mystery is revealed to us. As Victor Manuel Fernandez explains:

> We can find in the poor some profoundly Christian values: a spontaneous attention to the other, an ability to devote time to others and to go to another's aid without calculating time or sacrifice, while the more educated, with a more organized life, are unlikely to grant to others time, attention, and sacrifice spontaneously, with joy, and disinterestedly.[36]

In its effort to discover the *ethos* proper to the reality of a people's world, the theology of the people gathers input from four areas: "the reassessment of popular Catholicism, the contributions of the human and social sciences, the experiences of popular pastoral ministry, and the academic theological reflection that accompanies and guides pastoral praxis."[37] It is here that the sense of faith in peoples becomes relevant, for "faith critiques ideologies in their reductionist, totalizing, and absolutizing claims, whether those ideologies are conservative or revolutionary (of the Marxist or national-populist variety). But faith also takes on utopias without being identified with them, insofar as, through salvific discernment, they are open to the plenitude of the human, to the new in history, and to God. This discernment takes place in praxis, but also through it."[38] It is this sense of the faith of peoples that makes it possible to overcome the temptation of inconsequential academicism, which removes wisdom and mystery from theological endeavor, reducing it to mere scholarship.

Francis brings fresh air to the life of the Church and to social consciousness. He opens the door to a new era, inviting us to turn an ethical gaze toward the other, the poor, the excluded, the ones who *have no possibility of having possibilities.* We can note what he said at the *Te Deum* held in the cathedral in Buenos Aires in 2003, ten years before being elected pope:

> We have no right to indifference or disinterest or looking the other way. We can't "go on our way" as they did in the parable [of the Good Samaritan]. We have a responsibility for the wound that is the nation and its people. A new stage is beginning today, marked very deeply by frailty: frailty of our poorest and most excluded poor brothers and sisters, frailty of our institutions, frailty of our social bonds... Let us care for the frailty of our wounded people! Each with his wine, his oil, and his beast of burden.[39]

This new stage, now not only in society but in the Church as well, calls for return to a sense of the people. It demands that we struggle for recognition of their sociocultural place and reestablish with the people the social and ecclesial bonds that, having been broken in our recent history, have led nations to both economic ruin and to moral deterioration. It is an ethical call to heal *the wounded people*, often abused by various types of ideology, and with the people to recreate entire societies on the basis of inclusion and participation.

Sensus populi *and sociocultural location*

Pedro Trigo reminds us that "liberation theology proposes, as something new in history grounded in the Gospel, the constitution of the people as agent in history in both society and the Church."[40] The people are understood as an agent capable of creating and guiding history. The proper hermeneutic of popular culture means that speaking *of the poor* is at the same time speaking *of the people*, or poor people, for in them there is no place for a notion of the individual as an absolute and closed entity that does not live or understand itself in terms of its relationship to others. How then are we to understand the poor? What does being a poor people mean? Lucio Gera explains:

> When we speak of the poor we are thinking of human beings situated in their social and economic (or possibly other type of) condition, which makes them experience their lack of power... Being poor ultimately implies a moral condition the basic characteristic of which is humble openness to others, to God, and to human beings... The experience of being unable leads the poor to feel the need for other human beings, the need to ask, to claim, and to demand of others, of those who have power, the justice and the sympathy due to them. The first condition for belonging to a people is *the consciousness of needing others*, and this is, in the poor, an living and wounded consciousness. They are therefore more capable of being in solidarity—of giving to others and expecting from them—more capable of being in a people... Hence, we lean toward designating as people the multitude of the poor.[41]

This living *in-and-from* an understanding of shared life, which arises out of the radical condition of feeling the need of other human beings, frames what we are calling the sense of the people. Theologically, we agree with Victor M. Fernandez, for whom "speaking of a *sensus populi* is richer than speaking of a *sensus fidelium*. The subject of the *sensus fidelium* could be simply the sum of individuals who believe the same truths. By contrast, the *sensus populi* has a community subject, the people, which out of common Christian experience expresses itself by producing its own proper and specific culture and which provides others access to this same experience: the people evangelizes the people."[42] The *sensus populi* entails a sociocultural soteriology of a communal nature, hinted at by Francis in *Evangelii Gaudium* in the following terms: "God, in Christ, redeems not only the individual person, but also *the social relations existing between people*" (*EG* 178). In other words, and following the spirit of the council, we are not saved outside of the world, but in it, because everything having to do with development and human liberation also has to do with the Kingdom of God (*GS* 34; 38). But this does not mean being in the world as a kind of abstract, natural notion. Rather, it means being immersed in the web of sociocultural relations comprising the world,[43] in the midst of the life stories being woven by the characters, personalities, and options of persons. Methodologically, "making use of the mediation of historico-cultural analysis (in addition to socioanalytic mediation) and in particular of the conception of people and popular praxis (as an alternative to the notion of 'people-as-class'), contributed to highlighting the specific theological accent of the Argentine strand within the main current of Latin American liberation theology."[44] This methodological option differentiated it from the other liberation theologies arising in Latin America.

It is true that the poor live a daily nightmare of the soul as a consequence of the exclusion and powerlessness to which they are subjected. However, they respond to this reality not with frustration or violence but from the standpoint of their religious experience. They are people who want to attain the status of people-as-nation, citizens with full rights and duties, but first and primarily as faithful-people, because it is the religious realm that provides them with meaning, unity, hope, and encouragement to keep struggling. Understanding this reality requires overcoming a "handout" attitude on the part of the Church's pastoral structures and moving to a model of inculturation of the Gospel, a model that responds to the *ethos* of shared life or culture of encounter. Discovering the culture of encounter that underlies the life-world of the people makes it possible to comprehend that morality is no longer guided by the criteria of what is politically correct, conventional, or established, but by a spontaneous moral wisdom that leads to true discernment of the everyday—beyond legalism and pharisaism—and to the seeking of a good greater than the immediate:

> One can see that the poor people, even though they comply little or badly with some aspects of Christian morality due to the factors constraining them, nevertheless have complied much more than the highly educated with other aspects of morality: first, a spontaneous (sign of authenticity) and firm trust in God and a spirit of deep adoration; in addition, a sense of solidarity that is also spontaneous, that does not need motivations to get it moving, as usually occurs with the more educated.[45]

How has such a way of life and moral approach to reality come about? Popular culture, today primarily urban, has been the result of a process based on a massive exodus from the countryside. It is within that very process that the distinctive sociocultural features of the people have been formed. As Pedro Trigo explains:

> It hadn't been a planned exodus. They all went on their own. They had to invade a piece of land to build their own house themselves, get a job and eventually achieve relative stability... struggle for basic services, manage to advance their family, have some of their children even graduate from the university, find some faithful friends, and little by little build an understanding of what had happened to them, what was still happening, and form general ideas of the world and life. Doesn't this concrete human way of producing life constitute a culture?[46]

Does such an approach represent a populist theology? Does "populist" mean the same thing as "popular"? This isn't about defending an ideology or idealizing the poor, but rather about recognizing and preserving a specific human way of producing life, in short, a culture.

First, "the term 'people' is distinguished from the word 'mass,' because it assumes a collective subject capable of generating its own processes in history. They may be given some help, they may be aided in undertaking a path to education and maturity, but by assisting them to develop the best that God has given them, respecting their identity and style."[47] Or, as Justino O'Farrell puts it, the people "represents a concrete entity, or rather, a collective or political subject of history, capable of assuming the good of all as a common and lasting value."[48]

Second, the notion of people situates us in front of an outcry, the scandalous fact of inequity, of having to recognize that there is now talk of "different worlds within our one world: the First World, the Second World, the Third World, and at times the Fourth World" (Pope John Paul II, *Sollicitudo Rei Socialis* [*SRS*] 14) and that therefore the unfortunate "imperialist temptation" (*SRS* 22; 37)—which seeks only to level out and impose a single criterion and way of doing things—remains prevalent. Dire poverty, inequality, and the idolatry of money can be overcome if we are committed to the common good and, as we said previously, willing to set out on the path of "the option or love of preference for the poor. This is an option, or a special form of primacy in the exercise of Christian charity" (*SRS* 42), which is inspired by the golden rule: "Do to others whatever you would have them do to you" (Mt 7:12). As Francis said during his apostolic visit to the United States:

> Let us treat others with the same passion and compassion with which we want to be treated. Let us seek for others the same possibilities that we seek for ourselves. Let us help others to grow, as we would like to be helped ourselves. In a word, if we want security, let us give security; if we want life, let us give life; if we want opportunities, let us provide opportunities. The yardstick we use for others will be the yardstick that time will use for us.[49]

When Pope Francis uses the term "people," he does so with three meanings: people-as-poor, people-as-nation, and people-as-faithful. People-as-poor means those who are marginalized and excluded from the channels of sociopolitical and economic participation. This is the preferential sociocultural location of the Church, from which it will be able to generate processes of integration for building the people-as-nation, but it will do so journeying with the people-as-faithful, out of their beliefs and values, out of their faith and their struggles. In the Argentina of the 1970s, this meant "the shirtless and workers." This phrase refers to those who have no real possibilities of development because their life conditions are marked by dire poverty, by exclusion because they are outside the system. They constitute the majority of humankind, and they are the most affected by the current global development system.

Francis believes that, in a world overwhelmingly marked by impoverishment and lack of intercultural processes, each people creates its own culture, is protagonist of its own history, and should be respected as its own agent of evangelization (*EG* 122), for it constitutes a group of persons based on a common culture united by a single history with a collective life project.[50] "This entails appreciating the poor in their goodness, in their experience of life, in their culture, and in their ways of living the faith" (*EG* 199). Francis follows Rafael Tello in speaking of the need for the *people to evangelize the people* as a sign of a true inculturation. In this theology, the privileged realm for knowing the poor is thus not the political, because that is also a product of culture,[51] but the way in which the members of a people interrelate among themselves, their values and beliefs, their culture as "God's faithful people" (*EG* 125).

Encountering the soul of a people

How are we to become familiar with the people, with their true values and the way in which they live and shoulder the burdens of their everyday life, when there are so many prejudices deriving from cultural divisions and barriers and ideologies existing among the members of the same society? How, if we are unable to connect with the people, are we to listen to their soul, to what moves them and gives them meaning day by day by helping them make their daily burdens more bearable? The sociocultural location par excellence for doing so is that of the people's religion or religious life. This is the mediation most proper to a popular hermeneutics, because it is the place where everyday life becomes an experience of ongoing transcendence, of a wager in faith for life. In notes from the working meetings of COEPAL Lucia Gera observes:

> We have a foreign religion that may be Italian, Spanish, German, or whatever. This means that a renewal of the Church along these lines, that is, an application of Medellín, means being freed from religious— that is, foreign—subjection in some fashion. It means gaining independence from the cultural forms with which our religion is imbued, forms that are neither national nor of the people. Let us at least say this, even if it is simplistic: retrieving the hidden, original, national forms of religious expression. I wonder whether from here we may not be able to seek a certain unity in Medellín.[52]

In taking on reality in faith, the people become a *faithful people*, as Francis says, people who "express the faith in their own language, and who show their deepest feelings of sadness, uncertainty, joy, failure, and thanksgiving in various devotions: processions, votive lights, flowers, and hymns. All of these are beautiful expressions of their faith in the Lord and their love for his Mother, who is also our Mother."[53] Popular religion is hence the suitable means for comprehending the people's values, struggles, and conflicts, their hopes and yearnings, and for grasping the strength that accompanies them as they discern and process their everyday situation. Indeed, these expressions of popular religion are places for perceiving God's presence. Hence for Francis they acquire a theological status: "The way we listen to God the Father is how we should listen to his faithful people. If we do not listen in the same way, with the same heart, then something has gone wrong."[54]

It is out of this experience that the *ethos* proper to popular culture, its soul, may be grasped, as Bergoglio put it very clearly in Buenos Aires in 1999:

> Our people have soul, and because we can speak of the soul of a people, we can speak of a hermeneutic, a way of seeing reality, a consciousness. Today, enmeshed in conflicts, this people teaches us that we need not heed those who seek to distill reality into ideas, the lackluster intellectuals and ethicists without goodness, but that we must appeal to the depth of our dignity as people, appeal to our wisdom, appeal to our cultural reserves. It is a true revolution, not against a system, but internal, a revolution of memory and tenderness: memory of the great heroic founding deeds...and memory of the simple deeds on which we were nursed in the family.[55]

Thus, in *Evangelii Gaudium* Francis brings into the universal teaching of the Church this notion that comes from Latin American theology, specifically the theology of the people: *the soul of a people*, also called *popular mystique* or profound meaning/spirit of a people, as hermeneutic locus of popular culture. He thereby poses the challenge of creating an unbreakable unity between the popular reality—its culture and life-world—and "scholars and workers, businesspeople and artists, in a word, everyone" (*EG* 237), because the mystique we live and learn in the peoples becomes a new locus, where the sociocultural also becomes theological (*EG* 126). That mystique requires willingness and provides encouragement for discerning the merciful pathway of the God of life, who calls us to promote social change, to "feel God's saving pathway in view of 'true development, which is the pathway for each and all, from conditions of life that are less human to those that are more human'" (*Medellín* 6).

This entails a shift in the current way of being Church, because the assumption now is that the most appropriate place of ecclesial presence—both pastoral and academic—is that of being in the midst of the *poor peoples*, serving them and taking a stand with them in their struggles and hopes (*GS* 1) from the different positions in which we may find ourselves. This is what Francis does geopolitically, for example. The ecclesiastical institution, in what it is and does, is called to let itself be evangelized by the humanity that springs from the popular mystique, for it "receives in its own way the entire Gospel and embodies it in expressions of prayer, fraternity, justice, struggle and celebration" (*EG* 237). These are the ways in which the poor, the humblest, relate to God in their common vicissitudes and yearnings, and not only on the basis of individual needs.

In the popular mystique we find the Gospel inculturated in a continual desire to discern the pathway of the Spirit in the midst of the dramatic situations that surround us and that sometimes seem impossible to resolve. All these expressions or manifestations—prayer, brother/sisterliness, justice, struggle, and celebrations—become true theological loci, for, in addition to being forms of worship, they are intimate experiences that overflow into solidarity, into the need for social justice, into a way of living one's own situation in a hope that springs from a personal relationship with God that is trusted and celebrated jointly with others. In other words, in the following of Jesus the believer's suffering is identified with the suffering of Christ, crucified and impotent, but ever on the way toward a better future. This experience in which the daily is lived in the presence of mystery reveals the deep unity between history and salvation, between world and faith. As Rafael Tello says:

> For European and Spanish culture, Christianity was primarily salvation-oriented; for Indo-American culture, religion is what immediately shapes the life of human beings, and only then does it become salvation-oriented, because the life of human beings needs to be saved...The theological virtues lift human vitality toward the divine life, not destroying, but in fact enhancing it.[56]

The task of taking on the sociocultural location of the world of popular culture involves corresponding theological and pastoral issues, which opens the academy to new areas of discussion. Most important, however, it restores a sense of unity, lost to enlightenment reason, between theory and praxis, between scholarship and holiness, between theology and ministry. As Pope Francis noted in his message to the International Theological Congress held at the Catholic University of Argentina on the occasion of the hundredth anniversary of the school of theology:

> Catholicity requires, and calls for, a tense polarity between the particular and the universal, between the one and the many, between the simple and the

complex. To eliminate this tension goes against the life of the Spirit. Any attempt, any effort to reduce communication, to break the relationship between received Tradition and concrete reality jeopardizes the faith of the people of God. To consider either of the aspects unimportant is to place ourselves in a labyrinth that will not bring life to our people. Fracturing this communication will easily lead us to turn our gaze, our theology, into ideology.[57]

In this sense, the teaching of Francis presents, as an urgent task, the need to guide evangelization efforts toward building sociocultural bonds and to redirect ongoing history in a humanizing direction. To that end, the formation of civic consciousness and support for social forces and movements are key. They must be geared toward attaining a culture of encounter, in which we will find this soul of the people, their yearnings and struggles to grow in humanity.

Accompanying, promoting, and reflecting on these processes of change are not tasks foreign to the theologian or the evangelizer; they are part of the movement of inculturation of the Gospel, because, in the words of the pope spoken on his arrival in Bolivia on July 8, 2015, "fraternal charity, the living expression of the new commandment of Jesus, is expressed in programs, works, and institutions that work for the integral development of the person, as well as for the care and protection of those who are most vulnerable. We cannot believe in God the Father without seeing a brother or sister in every person." We cannot be Christian without reestablishing our bonds—personal, academic, or professional—in close encounter with the poor, with their way of being, in a *closeness* that humanizes our life and endows with transcendence the complex web of our relationships. Otherwise, our gaze will be reduced to an ethicist, academistic, and trivializing deception, guided by the spirit of superficial individualism that permeates hypermodern contemporary society. Hence, rescuing the soul of a people and healing its wounds poses a challenge to sophisticated society. Again, in the words of the pope:

> Reestablishing our social bonds with hope: this isn't a cold principle derived from ethics and reason. It doesn't mean a new and unachievable utopia, let alone a disaffected and exploitive pragmatism. It is the pressing need to *share life in order to jointly build the possible common good*, that of a community which yields its particular interests in order to share with justice its possessions, its interests, its social life in peace. Nor is it a matter of merely the administrative or technical management of a plan. Rather, it is a constant conviction which is expressed in deeds, in personal closeness, in a distinctive manner expressing *this willingness to change how we relate, kneading in hope a new culture of encounter, of closeness*, where privilege is no longer an unassailable and irreducible power, where exploitation and abuse are no longer a habitual way of surviving. Along these lines of fostering closeness, a culture of hope that creates new bonds, I invite you to win over, persuade, reassure, and convince.[58]

In view of the processes of inequality and exclusion that we experience, the recovery of social bonds and connection with peoples and their cultures stands as one of the most urgent challenges we face today. Thus, in the words of Francis, "it is a matter of hearing the cry of entire peoples, the poorest peoples of the earth, since 'peace is founded not only on respect for human rights, but also on respect for the rights of peoples'" (*EG* 190). It is the right to exist, a right that belongs to all peoples and their cultures, the right to simply preserve their soul and their own identity, that is today in jeopardy because of the leveling forces of globalization, financial totalitarianism, and pervasive individualism that dominate the mindset of so many in our societies. This is what Francis has been censuring through his new approach to geopolitics.

What is at stake in cultural globalization?

What we have been discussing thus far leads us to the question: What is really at stake in the current crisis of contemporary society? The answer can be found in the problem of globalization, the framework that defines the current age and in which both the task of theology and the discernment of Christian styles of life are posed anew.

We believe that globalization has been transformed into a fanatic ideology,[59] feeding into a single kind of thought, a homogenizing sociocultural mode that has been marketed as absolute and that excludes any possible alternative. This model, which we may call the prevailing model, is creating a new subculture modeled on the fluctuating parameters of the corporatized market. Today those who make up consumer society are treated as one-dimensional and robbed of their communal, pluricultural humanity; the human subject comes to be considered as a tradable and interchangeable good, and cultures as replaceable ways of life. In his 1961 article "Universal Civilization and National Cultures," Paul Ricoeur described this type of cultural globalization:

It can be said that throughout the world an equally universal way of living unfolds. This way of living is manifested by the unavoidable standardization of housing and clothing. These phenomena derive from the fact that ways of living are themselves rationalized by techniques which concern not only production but also transportation, human relationships, comfort, leisure, and news programming as well. Let us also mention the various techniques of elementary culture or, more exactly, the culture of consumption; there is a culture of consumption of worldwide dimensions, displaying a way of living which has a universal character.[60]

In light of this it is possible to visualize the more serious damage that this phenomenon causes in the destruction of what gives meaning to the people's ways of life, namely their cultures, those constructs that bear what, paraphrasing Ricouer, could be called the *ethical and mythical core of humanity*. In Ricoeur's words:

The phenomenon of universalization, while being an advancement of mankind, at the same time constitutes a sort of subtle destruction, not only of traditional cultures, which might not be an irreparable wrong, but also of what I shall call for the time being the creative nucleus of great civilizations and great cultures, that nucleus on the basis of which we interpret life, what I shall call in advance the ethical and mythical nucleus of mankind.[61]

This model translates into a geopolitical vision that tends to absolutize a center over all the rest, which it regards as periphery. It is a new form of imperialism that seeks to export a cultural pattern of being and living for everyone alike. From the standpoint of this absolute reality, defined as the center, everything deemed peripheral or different can be discarded. Hence there are more and more poor people, and the inequality gap widens, because the number of people living on the peripheries keeps growing and, with ever less access to the center and its services, they end up being not only displaced but completely excluded from the system.

In this overall framework the ideological conflicts between liberal capitalism and Marxist collectivism are left behind. The new polarity is situated between the current dominant direction of neoliberal-style globalization and the denial of any other possible humanizing alternative. Thus the social question of this age posed from the perspective of the theology of the people is set within the following parameters:

a) socioeconomically, by the existence of relations of ever more obvious exclusion in the face of growing inequality;

b) culturally, by the need to move from the pluricultural to the intercultural; and

c) sociopolitically, by the urgency of supporting the emerging forms of civil society, that is, the new social movements (neo-communitarianisms) and volunteer organizations, and so forth, which represent forces of change other than the state and the market and propose a more humane view of this world.

There is a pressing need to desacralize financial globalization and to de-ideologize its "uniformizing" cultural form. We need to move toward an alternative type of globalization, one that is polycentric, that recognizes the peripheries and from them can build new modes of relationship between the global and the local.[62] Such a model will enable new relationships of interdependence between persons, cultures, and states, not on the basis of new forms of colonialism, but rather on the basis of bonds of mutual solidarity and reconnection.

If this narrative is to overcome the current direction, it cannot reduce the notion of human rights to the rights of individuals alone, but must also extend it to peoples and their cultures as a whole.[63] This is the great challenge posed by the sociopolitical teaching of Francis and what he has been saying and doing through his apostolic journeys.

Recovering cultural rights

To grasp what this means, we must ask ourselves what we understand by culture and what relevance it has in shaping the geopolitical vision and pastoral action of Francis. What is at stake when we speak of cultural globalization?

In the words of Lucio Gera:

> Human beings cultivate, that is, they bring about their relationships with different realities, with them all: the material world, other human beings, and God. Culture is that activity which places the human being in human relationship with other realities and that human beings themselves perform. But in performing this activity in reference to other realities, they achieve themselves. In reaching fulfillment in relation to realities, they fulfill themselves, they develop, and they perfect themselves. Culture is understood as self-perfecting, as the activity by which

human beings achieve more fully human levels of life.[64]

Culture, then, is something organic. Again, following Gera: "It is something vital, it is a totality that comes from certain deep roots of life. Culture is the life of peoples and human beings. It is precisely thus because it is a matter of living and acting out of the ultimate depths of the subject, and an ongoing assimilating of subjects within themselves, toward their roots."[65] This understanding of culture took hold at Vatican II and brought about an epochal shift. The council understood culture not only as a source of creation in history and of social and ethnic diversity but also and most of all as a right:

> The duty most appropriate for our times, especially for Christians, is that of working diligently for fundamental decisions to be taken in economic and political affairs, both on the national and international level, which will everywhere recognize and satisfy the right of all to a human and social culture in conformity with the dignity of the human person without any discrimination based on race, sex, nation, religion, or social condition.[66]

The pastoral constitution *Gaudium et Spes* defines culture in its constitutively anthropological and plural sense. Therefore, speaking of culture entails speaking of cultures, that is, "the historical milieu which enfolds the people of every nation and age and from which they draw the values that permit them to promote civilization."[67] Culture is the source of fulfillment and re-creation of human beings, and hence it expresses what Ricoeur called "the ethical and mythical nucleus" of humanity.

Thus, for the council, recognizing and preserving the value of cultures means understanding that "people are defined first of all by their responsibility to their brothers and sisters and to history,"[68] and this responsibility is exercised through "different styles of life and multiple scales of values [that] arise from the diverse manner of using things, of laboring, of expressing oneself, of practicing religion, of forming customs, of establishing laws and juridic institutions, of cultivating the sciences, the arts and beauty."[69] Thus, preserving and developing cultural diversity is a duty incumbent on all human beings because it expresses something that is proper to them and innate in them, something that endows them with meaning in the midst of their everyday situation.

Culture cannot be spoken of in the singular because "concretely and historically, culture consists of cultures, in the diverse and particular ways that . . . peoples, in accordance with their proper disposition and historical experience, engage in their own endeavor of humanization. The social aspect of culture becomes prominent here. The peoples are its proper subject; the human person, of course, but in his or her social dimension. Here the way is also opened to the vision of culture in its historical dimension, understood not only as movement of an abstract becoming, but as a real process of the concrete history of people."[70] In this manner and not otherwise, cultures bear a natural right that demands their preservation and development; it is cultures that guarantee over time the historical processes that make us human beings.

The spirit of Vatican II was received and developed even further in the *Puebla Final Document*, inspired by the thought of Lucio Gera, who speaks of culture not as an add-on to the human being, but as an inalienable right on which depends the very realization of his or her psychic and physical condition. It is the locus of possibility and framework of fulfillment. Gera holds that "the idea of culture as disposition, prior to activity, but which inclines to act in a particular direction, makes it clear that it is like the 'co-naturalization' of a specific way of acting."[71] Therefore, to do away with culture is to rob human subjects of meaning, that is, *to incapacitate them as subjects*, to take away their rootedness and social belonging, to deconstruct their human subjectivity and consciousness. It is culture that allows human subjects *to be* in a specific way; culture supplies the conditions for them to develop in this world.[72]

As far back as 1968, UNESCO sponsored a meeting of experts on cultural rights and human rights. It was the first international seminar on cultural rights in which an official appeal was made to recognize and respect local cultures, integrating the historical past with the creative effort of the present, inasmuch as "culture is an inalienable human right which imbues all aspects of life." This was stated in opposition to the then growing tendency to favor "a universal, world civilization" characterized by "the eruption of technology into the remotest corners of the world." The document published at the conclusion of the seminar noted that it appeared "impossible to arrest the process by which ways of life and habits of behavior and appearance are standardized, even down to food and clothing."[73] In the face of the phenomenon of globalization it was believed that only the path of "preservation of native cultures" would allow "the struggle against the homogenization of the ways of life and superfluous values brought by mass culture."[74]

Then, in 2001, UNESCO took another step forward on this path by enacting the *Universal Declaration on Cultural Diversity*, stating in article 5 that "cultural rights are an integral part of human rights, which are universal, indivisible and interdependent," because "creation draws on the roots of cultural tradition, but flourishes in contact with other cultures. For this reason, heritage in all its forms must be preserved, enhanced and handed on to future generations as a record of human experience and aspirations, so as to foster creativity in all its diversity and to inspire genuine dialogue among cultures."[75]

Here the expression "cultural rights" refers to the relationship existing between worldwide and local culture in terms of the "generative complementarity of human totality in process."[76] They are rights bearing meaning that seek to preserve "the creative capacity of every human being."[77] As Ricoeur argues, "only a living culture, at once faithful to its origins and ready for creativity on the levels of art, literature, philosophy, and spirituality, is capable of sustaining the encounter with other cultures—not merely of sustaining but also of giving meaning to that encounter."[78]

However, the current tendency to absolutize the homogenizing global model jeopardizes that which gives identity and meaning to the life of persons, namely *the belonging and rootedness* of peoples in their specific cultures. The challenge is not one of delineating and observing the physical borders of national territories, but of preserving mindsets and vital impulses. The current model turns personal existence into a sad process of meaningless, unrelenting adaptation merely to survive. In opposing the dominant tendency that brings us to cultural homogenization,[79] Pope John Paul II held to the absolute "value of human cultures," which "no external power has the right to downplay and still less to destroy," for "globalization must not be a new version of colonialism. It must respect the diversity of cultures, which, within the universal harmony of peoples, are life's interpretive keys. In particular, it must not deprive the poor of what remains most precious to them, including their religious beliefs and practices."[80] Against the leveling processes that it opposes, the Church proposes as an alternative "a globalized culture of solidarity."[81] The creation of such a culture entails overcoming the current "globalization of indifference," which seeks to turn us into indolent creatures "incapable of feeling compassion at the outcry of the poor, weeping for other people's pain, and feeling a need to help them, as though all this were someone else's responsibility and not our own."[82]

How are we to respond to what is going on in our world? What can we do in the face of the dominant tendency of our age, which leaves no room for other possibilities and ways of life? What are the new signs of our times, and how are we to discern them in the light of the Gospel so as to build a better, more human world, without exclusion, without extreme inequality? More than ever, *healing the age* means reconnecting with the life-world of the poor, with the despised and excluded, with those who don't fit in society, those who have no future—in short, with all those who are outside any system, whether economic or political, religious or ecclesial. It is here that we are confronted by the challenge of rethinking the option for the poor in terms of defending peoples and their cultures and of setting out on a path of response to the new signs of the times of our global age.

2

RESPONDING TO
THE NEW SIGNS OF THE TIMES

The loss of humanizing bonds and reference points

Our era needs to be healed, humanized anew. This is one of the keys to understanding the commitment of Francis and his papacy, a commitment shaped in response to the phenomenon of globalization that characterizes our world today. The dominant form of this globalization has arisen from a process of world expansion based on the increased flexibility of markets and the rapid development of scientific and technical knowledge. Many associate the development of globalization with employment opportunities, new technologies, and easy systems for investment. Nevertheless, today we suffer its *cultural consequences*, including the loss of local identities, growing inequality, xenophobic fragmentation, and the proliferation of wars, which have given rise to the greatest migration crisis ever on a worldwide scale. Thus, today, "globalization is not about what we all, or at least the most resourceful and enterprising among us, wish or hope *to do*. It is about *what is happening to us all*,[1] its broadest effects. "The deepest meaning conveyed by the idea of globalization is that of the indeterminate, unruly and self-propelled character of world affairs; the absence of a center, of a controlling desk, of a board of a directors, of a managerial office. Globalization is . . . the new world disorder."[2]

Globalization has produced a new kind of interdependence between all the countries in the Western hemisphere. Its origins can be found in a political and economic expansion driven by multinational companies and banks and by international financial agencies. The effect over time has been the standardization and homogenization of a model of world culture that leads to the loss of the specific identities of local peoples and erodes their creative capacity. Because these new relations of interdependence are antagonistic, they tend to prevent processes of symbiosis and interculturality. The changes resulting from unchecked globalization were criticized by the Latin American bishops when they met in Aparecida, Brazil, in 2007. Referring to indigenous communities, they noted that

> economic and cultural globalization jeopardizes their very existence as different peoples. Their gradual cultural transformation leads to rapid disappearance of some languages and cultures. Migration compelled by poverty is deeply influencing change of customs, of relationships, and even of religion.[3]

Certainly we all depend on one another. What happens in one place can have worldwide consequences, and our global decisions and policies can obviously affect local socioeconomic situations. But what we fail to do also influences the living conditions of people whom we will never know. Today we are suffering the sociocultural consequences of globalizing advances in knowledge, technology, and science. There are no more geographical limits, given the free movement of money and the failure of national states. The modern idea of sustained development, of global well-being for the whole human race, is today mere nostalgia, a vague desire that finds no foothold. This is because belief in the absolute value of human life has been lost, and the primacy of the subject-subject relationship has been replaced by that of subject-object or production-consumption.

This situation has its roots in activities that led to the absolutizing of the market and of the financial system, turning them into a fetish, something pseudo-sacred acting in the form of an invisible and extraterritorial power, a kind of faceless force with no ethical ties. The essence of this force is the utter freedom to invest in those countries that offer greater detachment from roots in the local, solely in order to obtain the highest possible profits. This is compounded by a kind of magic realism, likewise pseudo-religious, which presents the strange and foreign, the inhuman and distant, as the new everyday normal before which the only response is a lazy acceptance. Thus, the current dominant tendency offers no room for the transcendent value of everyday life as the proper place for reconnection with others, with creation, and with God.

Accompanying the collapse of geographical boundaries, the postmodern turn away from "strong thought" along with the decline in critical thinking, and the redefinition of relations of space and time, is a new way of being and acting, one based on virtual hypermobility, proper to today's hyper-postmodernity. There is no room here for yearnings for the former certainties, nor for the desires to construct new "wholes" or systems of thought. What stands out is the ephemeral, the trivial. The individual, the hedonistic, has been absolutized; the sense of the quotidian has been lost. Thus there has arisen a new mood in our age, one in which the void has gradually changed human subjectivity from an initial disenchantment with ideologies and political systems to a state of uprootedness and lack of sociocultural belonging. Because of hypermobility we live in neighborhoods as strangers and interpersonal relationships are relativized. In other words, we are far from the condition in which proximity to the other (as neighbor, someone close to me) serves as a transcendent value of the everyday. We are more inclined to foster virtual communities of common interests than spontaneous, gratuitous relationships capable of creating newness and meaning in our lives.

This new condition of human subjectivity, devoid of the everyday and of close ties, has been bringing about a "counter-power" with no territory or local foothold, nourished by antagonistic relationships that capitalize on a form of radical nihilism. If the realm of the private and individual is proclaimed as having absolute value, the effort to reconnect with others ceases to be a source of meaning. New local phenomena such as terrorism, xenophobia, and organized crime emerge, spread, and become worldwide. The notion of provisional and strategic networks replaces that of sustained humanizing relationships, and psychosocial polarization is used as a strategy for conquering sociopolitical spaces and redefining them ideologically. The struggle to survive nullifies the meaning of transcendence, thereby producing a profound existential disillusionment, given the impossibility of achieving our desires. Those desires themselves do not always draw inspiration from personalizing relationships and do not always favor growth in humanity, since they are nourished by antagonistic and trivial relationships that accentuate only what we lack vis-à-vis others. This produces a kind of psychosocial envy, one that is unable to add but can only subtract, that does not commit itself to the common good but only to individual satisfaction. What we see in the end is the paradox of wanting to live while avoiding a sense of *needing* the other in order to be oneself.[4]

One of the causes of this radical shift that affects the very construction of human subjectivity can be situated in what Max Weber calls the separation between economic activity and the network of mutual rights and obligations in which markets and local communities operate,[5] something that leads to the erosion of social and family bonds and the fostering of a narrow individualism. This forms a model of action that is no longer human but virtual, free of moral questioning and legal restraints, a model based on the formal rationality of an analytic and abstract nature on the one hand, and instrumental, functional, and procedural rationality on the other. There is no room here for the difference noted by Karl Jaspers between the remorse we feel when we directly harm other human beings (moral guilt) and the guilt that appears when the deed done to another is not directly related to our own personal action (metaphysical guilt). In other words, the lines separating accomplices, collaborators, spectators, and executioners are diluted in a kind of pharisaic observance of the legal framework in effect, but without its necessary correlate, morality. As Francis explains: "In the prevailing culture, priority is given to the outward, the immediate, the visible, the quick, the superficial and the provisional. What is real gives way to appearances. In many countries globalization has meant a hastened deterioration of their own cultural roots and the invasion of ways of thinking and acting proper to other cultures which are economically advanced but ethically debilitated."[6]

The upshot is a kind of absence of conscience, that is, of subjectivity itself, which allows one to live inured to any pain arising from the concrete reality of the other and the absolute value of life. We might speak of an inability to construct criteria of discernment. In this globalized era, the concrete and individual face of the one doing evil is not

seen, not identified, and therefore we seem to be facing a
society without limits, shielded from punishment, incapable
of assuming responsibility for any consequences. And yet,
since there are no moral innocents, we are not free of guilt.
One way or another, we are all complicit by action or omission in what happens or does not happen in our world. Evil,
of its essence, globalizes, and the only way to bear the situation without great personal trauma is by having a coma-
tose conscience.

The prevailing situation is radically unjust, not only because it oppresses and excludes but also because it leads to
dehumanization and the absence of meaning. In other
words, it renders the human being incapable of living in relationship, of constructing permanent personal bonds and
sociocultural bridges. The need to change this reality poses
an ethical imperative, because in our age, as described in
the *Aparecida Document* and as Francis has noted in his
speeches:

> one may note a kind of new cultural colonization by
> the imposition of artificial cultures, spurning local
> cultures and tending to impose a uniform culture in
> all realms. This culture is characterized by the self-
> reference of the individual, which leads to indiffer-
> ence toward the other, whom one does not need and
> for whom one does not feel responsible. There is a
> tendency to live day-by-day, with no long-term de-
> signs, and no personal, family, and community at-
> tachments. Human relations are regarded as goods of
> consumption, leading to emotional relations without
> responsible and final commitment.[7]

An economic system that kills

In a letter written for Lent, dated February 13, 2013, the then still cardinal Bergoglio described the effects of the globalization process and its major problems in the following terms:

> We are battered by the suffering of the innocent and peaceful; the contempt for the rights of weaker persons and peoples are not so distant from us; the imperialism of money with its demonic effects such as drugs, corruption, human trafficking—even of children—along with material and moral poverty, are common currency. The destruction of dignified work, painful emigrations and the lack of a future also join in this symphony. Nor are our mistakes and sins as Church outside this big picture."[8]

A month later, on March 13, 2013, he would be elected pope and take the name Francis, and this would mark the beginning of an unexpected turn in the journey of the Church in this twenty-first century.

On July 8 of that year, Francis suddenly decided, without even notifying the Vatican Secretariat of State, to make his first journey to the island of Lampedusa, in Italy, a place where the cry of the new victims of our age is poignantly heard and felt. These are the victims of a global system that has collapsed in crisis, a system that discards the poorest, those whose living conditions are marked by extreme poverty and exclusion, who know that they will never, under current conditions, find a safe and dignified place to flourish in our world. They are people destined to suffer the terrible subculture of struggling for survival, those whom the current system of globalization characterizes as disposable individuals, as expendable beings who can always be replaced by nameless others in the labor market.

They constitute the majority of humankind, and they are those most affected by the current system of global development. What is wrong is not a simple model or style of management, but the system itself, which absolutizes the financial and consumerist dimension of the economy. Though it is a system that has produced great wealth globally, it has done so at the cost of producing the highest levels of economic inequality and social exclusion in human history. This has turned the market into a *fetish*[9] and human subjects into underlings and slaves of consumption. Indeed, the poor are not simply those who *do not have*; they are those who *have no way of having*.[10] Hence, today more than ever, being poor means being excluded from everything, so that "the poor are not looked at, they aren't asked anything, they aren't even spoken to, they are not taken into account, for the majority they don't exist, that is, they are positively erased from their lifeworld."[11] Here we stand at the nerve center of Francis's concern for us to be converted to the poor, to turn our gaze toward their situation. The problem we face is not simply temporary, nor can it be easily resolved through aid policies or social volunteer actions. It is a structural problem, one that excludes the poor because they are poor and denies them the chance for a decent and sustainable life. That is what Francis critiqued in his second apostolic journey, which was to another Italian island, Sardinia. There, referring to this system, he said that "it isn't a problem only of Italy or some countries in Europe, it is the consequence of a worldwide choice, of an economic system that leads to this tragedy, an economic system which has at its center an idol, which is called money."[12]

Under the current state of affairs the vast majorities will have neither a future nor a decent life. They will not be able to enjoy the benefits of civilization such as democracy and human rights, nor will they know what it means to have satisfying work enabling them to become part of society, to be recognized as autonomous subjects capable of freely developing their highest human potential for the sake of the common good. This very serious reality has not come about by accident. It is the consequence of the prevailing way in which business and politics are carried out. In view of this situation, Francis asserts that it is no longer a model that produces some poor and excluded people, but is rather a system that produces hundreds of millions of poor people who will always live on the peripheries.

In other words, "Such an economy kills... because it is no longer simply about exploitation and oppression, but something new. Exclusion ultimately has to do with what it means to be a part of the society in which we live; those excluded are no longer society's underside or its fringes or its disenfranchised—they are no longer even a part of it. The excluded are not the 'exploited' but the outcast, the 'leftovers.'"[13] Zygmunt Bauman speaks of exclusion as the proper and intended action of the new Big Brother of our time—to use Orwellian language—which is responsible for "spotting the people who 'do not fit' into the place they are in, banishing them from that place and deporting them [to] 'where they belong,' or better still never allowing them to come anywhere near in the first place."[14]

In line with Bergoglio's last letter for Lent 2013, when he was still the archbishop of Buenos Aires, we may ask whether we have allowed ourselves to be influenced by a feeling of impotence, whether it makes sense to try to change this sad reality,[15] because after all the problem is not only social in nature, but anthropological and theological; it is about the loss of any bonds of belonging and sociocultural identity.[16] Nevertheless, it must be understood that the question of God can be raised only out of suffering for the other *as brother or sister*.[17] If human beings have lost their center, if they are no longer the subjects of creation received gratuitously from God, that same God reminds them of their roots, their most authentic calling, their relationship as brothers and sisters which gives meaning and transcendence to their being in the world. When this relationship is lost, all that remains is the pure naked desire for power by and for oneself, without the other. When brother/sisterhood suffers, the human dimension undergoes a sad transformation from its more genuine and real condition, and traits of indolence begin to appear, leading individuals to live only for themselves, based on the logic of their own personal survival.[18]

We need to align our hearts and options and be honest toward overall reality. The existence of poor people cannot be seen as a collateral effect or a necessary condition for opportunities to become available to others (as the established order claims). Instead, we must recognize that the growing number of poor people on this earth has a cause, and this cause reflects concrete decisions that point history in one direction or another.[19] We stand before the scandal of a global structural problem that reveals the ruthlessness of human indifference and the brutality of collective dehumanization. In fact, it is a problem that affects us all, insofar as we are brothers and sisters of one another, responsible for the common good of our societies. Hence, "as long as the problems of the poor are not radically resolved by rejecting the absolute autonomy of markets and financial speculation and by attacking the structural causes of inequality, no solution will be found for the world's problems or, for that matter, for any problems. Inequality is the root of social ills."[20] This dismal situation is well described in the accusation made by Pedro Trigo, which expresses the underlying anthropological problem—that of identity and belonging, of rootedness and development—which makes the option for the poor something essential in any stance for the human:

> The established order has no place for a decent life for most of the barrio: neither material space nor working conditions, nor recognition, nor services...It isn't simply that there's no place, but that the established order positively states that there isn't, that it is superfluous, that it would be better if they went away, that they will not find work, that they don't have the minimum requirements for getting married, that it is irresponsible for them to bring children into the world, that there are no places for them in hospitals, nor water, nor electricity for them, nor schools for their children, that they are parasites, that they ought to go somewhere else. That is, life is positively denied them. They are deprived of it.[21]

By way of the poor

What Francis proposes vis-à-vis this situation is not a mere change of focus in church pastoral work, or fresh language, or an updating of existing religious forms. He proposes a re-thinking of the way of being Church, so that it may honestly confront the grave effects of the structural crisis that it is living, and so that it may thereby return to the anthropological path traced by Vatican II, which taught that humans are by nature social beings (*GS* 12). For members of the Church, responsibility for others is not accidental or optional, but a necessary response to God's act in entrusting the other to us. As Lucio Gera explained in 1968 when speaking of the ecclesiological implications of the new spirit of the council:

> The mystery of God consists of his design in communicating and revealing himself to the human being, but also of giving us to the other, to our brothers and sisters. In the mystery of God is involved his will: that the other, the neighbor, obtains a presence and a manifestation in me, and hence that I discover that neighbor, and in some fashion be converted to my brother and sister.[22]

Thus, God's self-revelation is not an end in itself; it is the means by which God reveals that the mystery of the human being is manifested and fully achieved through our conversion to our brothers and sisters. It is only along this route that our belonging and identity as people of God is constructed, inasmuch as the "ecclesial relationship to the other is constitutive of the meaning and fullness of existence."[23]

This new universal mode of being Church, manifested in conversion to the other as brother/sister, is embodied in the route of the poor. This means that it is not enough to reconnect with the reality of the poor and their life-world if they are not also recognized as true agents of the Kingdom of God, people who can humanize us with their own values and gifts. It has to do with recovering a horizontal relationship with the life-world of the poor, a relationship that goes beyond mere charitable giving and becomes an axis centering and shaping every other personal, social, economic, political, and religious option that we make. It means opting for the poor to become not simply the addressees of a religious message or of economic beneficence but fully subjects in the Church and society. This mindset is what builds a new way of being for the Church. This new way of being is based on a preferential option for the poor—for those condemned to live on the socioeconomic and existential peripheries—and a recognition of the impact that they have in promoting conversion in all those who are part of the ecclesial institution and the community of the Church.

The desire of Francis that the Church be poor and for the poor follows directly from the reception of Vatican II (1962–1965) through the Second General Conference of Latin American Bishops meeting in Medellín (1968). In Europe Vatican II was received as political theology by Johann Baptist Metz, while in Latin America it was translated into liberation theology by Gustavo Gutiérrez, Ignacio Ellacuría, Jon Sobrino, and others. However, something special happened in Argentina, because the reception of Vatican II through Medellín was in turn embodied in the *Final Document of the Second Extraordinary Assembly of Argentine Bishops in San Miguel* (1969), as we noted earlier.

The new ecclesial era in which we live draws its inspiration from John XXIII's call for a church of the poor, as he stated in his September 11, 1962, radio address: "The Church presents itself as it is and as it wants to be, as Church of all, and in particular as the Church of the poor."[24] That is, a church that not only "knows how to see the miseries of life in society" but also recognizes that they are "unjust situations that God does not want," in which we must not be participants either by action or omission. A church which, as *Medellín* says, is "truly poor, missionary, and paschal, separate from all temporal power and courageously committed to the liberation of each and every man."[25] The foundation for this option is not pastoral but rather theological and incarnational, because it derives from the call to see "the face of Christ in every poor person, as his sacrament."[26] Or, as Paul says, we are to "always remember the poor" (Gal 2:10).

Another event that formed part of the process of reception of the council was the *Pact of the Catacombs* signed in Rome on November 16, 1965, when a group of bishops, including Dom Helder Cámara of Brazil, affirmed the need to return to the praxis of the Jesus of history by being "a servant and poor Church." In what did this vision consist? The pact proposed renouncing "the wealth, property, titles, privileges, and honors of the ecclesiastical institution,"[27] and urged living "according to the ordinary manner of our people."[28] Thus, the new ecclesial spirit would be marked by brother/sisterliness, justice, and compassion as the main thrusts of ecclesial praxis. The pact included a call to "to transform our works of welfare into social works based on charity and justice."[29] Thus, the bishops who signed the document understood that the option for the poor would mean treating them as agents, as authors of their own history, and not as beneficiaries and objects of piety. Accordingly, the ecclesial narrative had to join the struggle against the structural causes of poverty and take concrete action so that the poor might emerge from their economic and cultural misery.[30] For this group of bishops, the option was not to be based on isolated actions but on a joint exercise of collegiality, because "the collegiality of the bishops finds its supreme evangelical realization in jointly serving the two-thirds of humanity who live in physical, cultural, and moral misery."[31]

This ecclesial vision was picked up in Argentina in 1969 in the *San Miguel Document*, which proposes a poor church that not only lives in spiritual poverty or interior abnegation with regard to material goods but that assumes voluntary poverty—in other words, a church that renounces privileges, luxury, and honorific titles; a church that directs the management of property to serve the pastoral needs of the poorest, especially with regard to the church structures and the availability of personnel.[32]

The option for the poor as it has taken shape in Latin America proclaims, on the one hand, that when God sees the oppression of the Hebrews in Egypt, God responds with an offer of liberation. This is made quite clear in documents such as those of Medellín. On the other hand, it is understood that the meaning of that divine election is above all paschal, that in Jesus, God takes flesh in a divided society marked by oppression and takes a position, stands on the side of the poor, because it is they who bear the heaviest weight of suffering in the world, it is they who live overburdened and exhausted. It is to these poor that Jesus offers the possibility of carrying a lighter load. The consequence for everyone is clear: there is no salvation that does not include concrete actions to eradicate the evil inflicted by the majority of humankind on those who are economically poor and socioculturally excluded.

Being a poor church is the necessary prior condition for being a church of and for the poor; otherwise it will not be able to be a credible sign and sacrament capable of converting hearts. Indeed, as people of God it is called to mediate salvation through actions and gestures of liberation from everything that dehumanizes and divides its members. This is the sense in which Francis believes that unless the problems of the poor are addressed no one will do well because the problems of the world will not be resolved (*EG* 202).

As Pedro Trigo notes: "For the God of Jesus, the poor come before Christians: they are first, because only when things go well for the poor, will they go well for all... The consequence drawn by Jesus is that it is brotherly/sisterly service or its absence that determines our eternal fate (Mt 25:40–45)."[33] This is something that the pope has repeated insistently, and that in Medellín and Puebla was considered essential to the mission of the Church and to the vocation of the Christian. Sadly, this is what has been undermined by the primacy of private religion, the practice of inconsequential piety that is alien to the historical Jesus and his praxis.

This context of church life and reflection on the state of things in the world inspires in Pope Francis a theologico-pastoral option profoundly influenced by some of the main categories and methodology of liberation theology.[34] According to that theology, theological thought, pastoral praxis, the life of faith, and the mission and identity of the church institution may not be viewed as isolated fragments. For Pope Francis, correlative pairs like faith and sociopolitical life, or the academy and pastoral involvement, are not to be thought of separately, lest they foster a dysfunctional relationship between well-educated persons and the reality of the poor, to which all are morally indebted. The danger of a lightweight corporate Christianity is latent. Francis reminds us of this in *Laudato Si* when he speaks of those who "live and reason from the comfortable position of a high level of development and a quality of life well beyond the reach of the majority of the world's population" (49), and do not connect with the world of the poor or deal with them personally, resulting in a lack of connection with reality that serves only to "numb the conscience" (ibid.). By becoming poor and of the poor, the Church will no longer view unjust situations from the distance of its comfort, but from the closeness of one following "the Messiah of the poor"[35] in the hope "that an authentic example of abnegation and freedom of spirit by its consecrated members will lead the rest of the people of God to a similar path of poverty and a change of the prevailing individualistic mindset into another one of social sense and concern for the common good."[36]

At Medellín the question of *where* God is present was addressed in light of the partiality shown by Christ, who appears in a special manner through his relationships with the poor and poverty.[37] The poor, who are the majority of humankind, cry out for "a passage from less human to more human conditions."[38] Then at the third CELAM meeting in Puebla in 1979, light was shed on the other question, that of *how* God is present in our reality, with God located on the side of the poor, simply because they are poor and without any precondition whatsoever.[39] There is a reason why the poor were the first to experience the historic action of Jesus and learn of God's liberating revelation.

The social location recovered by Francis in the narrative of his magisterium evokes the salvation-history dimension of reality (*GS* 4) by grasping that, in this globalized era, the sign of the times par excellence is the sustained and ever greater impoverishment of the world and the ever-growing levels of inequality. This is a fact that challenges our conscience and our way of life. For Francis, this social location poses a decisive challenge to theology and to the understanding of reality as *theo*-logical—that is, as a primary *locus theologicus*, a place of revelation of God's presence, a place that exposes the historico-theological dimension of reality (*GS* 11). Thus it is not enough to consider the commonly accepted theological *loci*— tradition, magisterium, and scripture (*ubi*); one must live and think from the substantial reality (*quid*) itself (which determines all these *loci* and shapes their meaning and actuality), that is, from the reality of the poor in their struggle to humanize their social, economic, and political conditions of life.[40]

Taking on this cause is a structural option incumbent on all members of the Christian community, and it reveals the

character of our own humanity.[41] As Vatican II states in
Lumen Gentium: "The Church encompasses with love all
who are afflicted with human suffering, and in the poor and
afflicted it sees the image of its poor and suffering Founder.
It does all it can to relieve their need and in them it strives to
serve Christ."[42] The challenge is thus to rethink a church that
is called to "opt for the poor" in a manner that is free of cultural prejudice, religious indoctrination, and political ideology.[43] Care must be taken to avoid utilizing the poor, making
them into objects, recipients of public policies and religious
subject matter, or into replaceable and discardable merchandise of the economic realm.[44] The way of the poor thus leads
us away from elitism and a disconnection from reality. It is
certainly people-oriented and relational, but it is not populist, because it is not based on political theory. Rather, it is
based on the very mystery of the incarnation of God in the
midst of a concrete historical reality and a poor people, becoming incarnate as one more poor person, as Yahweh's poor.

The theological reading that emerges from Francis's
teaching holds that the "poor are a theological category" (*EG*
198), that in the poor "we see the face and the flesh of Christ,
who made himself poor so to enrich us with his poverty (cf.
2 Cor 8:9). The poor are the *flesh of Christ*."[45] This understanding of the poor is a *sine qua non* for Christian life, because what Jesus proposes, which is the Kingdom of God, is
not a private and intimate relationship with God (*EG* 183),
but a relationship that entails building a society of brother/
sisterliness, peace, justice, and dignity for all (*EG* 180).
Hence the option is not a choice for each individual that we
encounter on the road. It isn't a charitable action or an ideological position. It is primarily an option that has both a
structural (in that it entails socioeconomic change) and *structuring* dimension (in that it requires a change of "mindset")

of the entire life of Christians and the manner in which they relate to their faith vis-à-vis God and their brothers and sisters. What is at stake is a decent passage through life, which is what God willed for us when he created us. The option that has to do not with populism but with Christian ethics. It is not isolated individuals who are saved, but "social relations between human beings," that is, each one, but in relationship to the people with whom he or she lives (*EG* 178).

Both academic and pastoral theologians, along with intellectuals in general, are called to recognize and become inculturated—cognitively and socially—in their own poor people, in those milieus of exclusion, in order to really know their life-world, their culture. It is this option for the poor that makes it possible to build the true common good and achieve the momentum needed to arrive at a higher unity, that of the nation. At that level it will be possible to overcome the influence of outside ideologies, whether Marxist or liberal, socialist or capitalist, which seek only to destroy memory and identity and to level societies without taking into account the diverse cultures within them and the role of these cultures in promoting true values of humanization and development (*EG* 220).

A hermeneutic of social processes and movements

One of the aspects in the teaching of Francis that has encountered the greatest resistance has been his proposal that the option for the poor be a structural element in the life and mission of the entire Church, and hence capable of bringing about "real changes"[46] in society. Such a stance necessarily affects relations between the center and the peripheries, between Rome and local churches, between the Church and society at large. Under this scheme, changes of whatever nature cannot be driven from the center, but rather must come from the peripheries, whether existential and social or political and religious. This is the particular hermeneutic that Francis has applied to his entire magisterium. He himself explains it in the following terms: "The great changes in history were realized when reality was seen not from the center but from the periphery. It is a hermeneutical question: reality is understood only if it is looked at from the periphery, and not when our viewpoint is equidistant from everything."[47]

This means a shift from our zones of security and comfort toward the place where the excluded, the discarded of society are living. It is from there and with them that "the truth of reality" can be understood.[48] The displacement required means being converted, going to and being with the poor, where they live, knowing first-hand what people are experiencing, and not letting ourselves give in to the temptation presented by the prevailing system, which permits us to think about the reality of others but without knowing them or experiencing their life-worlds, their conditions. This is the risk brought about by a certain nominalism that permeates academia, producing specialists who have never had a real connection with the persons or the situations about which they write. Such was the explanation given by Francis in a 2014 interview with the Jesuit Antonio Spadaro:

> It is not a good strategy to be at the center of a sphere. To understand we ought to move around, to see reality from various viewpoints. We ought to get used to thinking. I often refer to a letter of Father Pedro Arrupe, who was General of the Society of Jesus. It was a letter directed to the Centros de Investigación y Acción Social (CIAS). In this letter, Father Arrupe spoke

of poverty and said that some time of real contact with the poor is necessary. This is really very important to me: the need to become acquainted with reality by experience, to spend time walking on the periphery in order really to become acquainted with the reality and life-experiences of people. If this does not happen we then run the risk of being abstract ideologists or fundamentalists, which is not healthy.[49]

Without this view from the periphery, the proclamation of the Gospel will be unsubstantial, unattractive, unable to get to the root of the true problems in order to remedy them.[50] Therefore it is a matter of changing our location, of opting to live on the peripheries. This option does not consist of providing programs of instruction and religious formation, or setting up charitable works of social assistance. It requires going beyond mere assistance to establishing a *loving attention* that regards poor people as subjects in a horizontal relationship, treating them equally.[51] The loving attention that Francis talks about entails a change in life-direction, of the way everything is done, so that others—the poor—may have a decent life. We see this kind of attention being given by those "priests and pastoral workers [who] carry out an enormous work of accompanying and promoting the excluded throughout the world, alongside cooperatives, favoring businesses, providing housing, working generously in the fields of health, sports and education."[52] Their incentive is not from an ideology or a social program, but from the heart of the Gospel, from the right that we all have to "live well."[53]

This is not a new idea in Francis's thought. As background, we may recall Bergoglio's experience with the *villa* (slum) priests in Buenos Aires, who were linked to the Third World Priests Movement and supported by bishops Enrique

Angelelli and Eduardo Pironio, as well as others. A year into his papacy, Francis was asked about these priests, such as Father Carlos Mujica, who was murdered in 1974. His answer was, "They're not communists but priests who struggle for social justice." The key to this interpretation can be found in the unity of three themes—social justice, theology, and pastoral action—because, as Francis said in Santa Cruz, there is "a system that . . . continues to deny many millions of our brothers and sisters their most elementary economic, social and cultural rights. This system runs counter to the plan of Jesus."[54] What, then, can the Church do to struggle against everything that produces poverty and oppression?

The theologico-pastoral path of Francis calls the universal magisterium to live the Church's mission from within the *new historical processes of social change that serve the struggles of the poor majorities* for a better world, one that is more brother/sisterly and livable. We are not talking about processes offered by the ecclesiastical institution through its pastoral action. What is being proposed is that the ecclesial institution recognize, take on, and promote those processes—including those of non-Christian persons and groups—that have a humanizing aim in society as a whole, and that are moving against the tide of the contemporary process of globalization. One of the most novel and specific modes for embodying this vision is the one that Francis has put in practice by inviting, accompanying, and promoting social movements that are leading processes in history. He said as much at the First World Meeting of Popular Movements: "Such proactive participation transcends the processes of formal democracy. Moving toward a world of lasting peace and justice calls us to go beyond paternalistic forms of assistance; it calls us to create new forms of participation that include popular movements . . . They are a real sign of the inclusion of the excluded in the building of a common destiny."[55]

These movements reveal that "the poor not only suffer injustice, they also struggle against it,"[56] and the duty of the Church, in fidelity to the Reign of God, lies in "accompanying them suitably on their path of liberation" (*EG* 199). Indeed, the Church must do so *from within the particular ways in which these movements understand and carry out their struggles.* This is where the primacy of the periphery over the center becomes real: in the transition from one model of Church that has been accustomed to determining the directions and modes of change to another model of Church—people of God—that recognizes what already exists in secular history in order to take it on and strengthen it. In other words, "The Church cannot and must not remain aloof from this process in its proclamation of the Gospel," because "respectful cooperation with popular movements can revitalize these efforts and strengthen processes of change."[57]

The importance of popular movements is that they evangelize the Church, they help it to be converted. They are part of the process of pastoral conversion that the institution must take on. They teach us that the Church ought to be at the service of everyone, not only of its members, for if it wishes to really foster a culture of encounter it cannot limit itself to gathering those who are already part of its structure, nor believe that anyone who is not in it must eventually become part of it. The periphery has its own life, its own particularity and dynamic, which must be respected as something that contains the presence of the Word. At the First World Meeting of Popular Movements, Francis expressed this insight in the following terms:

> I know that you are persons of different religions, trades, ideas, cultures, countries, continents. Here and now you are practicing the culture of encounter,

so different from the xenophobia, discrimination and intolerance that we witness so often. Among the excluded, one finds an encounter of cultures where the aggregate does not wipe out the particulars.[58]

Although this way of understanding the relationships of the Church with the world is novel in the universal magisterium, it is not so in the life of the Latin American Church. In the late 1960s, Gustavo Gutiérrez was already talking about the need for a prophetic ministry and the incorporation of the social forces of change into the Church's pastoral action. In his well-known reflections on pastoral paths for the Church in Latin America he noted that pastoral ministry is based on a "theology of salvation which draws the logical consequences from the claim that all human beings have been saved by Christ, that is, that all human beings have the same possibilities for salvation, whether they are in the church or not," or are Christians or not.[59] He went on to point out that that "if it is said that salvation is obtained due to a behavior of personal abnegation, of generous commitment to others, of charity, it is clear that chances of salvation are equal to all human beings, believers or atheists."[60]

Thus the Church has to overcome the temptation to salvation exclusivism, to feeling that it possesses salvation and is the center of history. It cannot keep proposing a self-referential pastoral practice aimed at bringing people in society into religious groupings. The challenge today lies in taking on the secular world as world and living—following the spirit of Vatican II—as people of God in the midst of the peoples of this world, an outgoing Church learning to respond to the new signs of the times and not to its own needs or bureaucratic interests.[61]

The fundamental soteriological principle of a Church going out of itself lies in understanding that "those who enter into communion with God are those who are in communion with human beings."[62] It does not go out to occupy new spaces; we are not in a situation of initial evangelization. The reason for going out is to bring about new alternative and horizontal processes in history, and to do that by first going where people are and becoming familiar with their life-worlds. Here is how the pope explains it:

> I like the image of a "process," where the drive to sow, to water seeds that others will see sprout, replaces the ambition to occupy every available position of power and to see immediate results. Each of us is just one part of a complex and differentiated whole, interacting in time: peoples who struggle to find meaning, a destiny, and to live with dignity, to "live well."[63]

Sustaining this vision is also Lucio Gera with his theology of processes in history,[64] which seeks to identify the major events of an era, those that mark its historical direction, and to discern in them certain signs of the times that reveal the meaning of salvation,[65] guiding people toward universal brother/sisterliness as the horizon of Spirit's activity in history.[66] So where are these signs manifested today? According to Gera, and also to Francis, and following the direction of Latin American theology, they are manifested in the new processes of history that in our time are struggling against the prevailing system of globalization, centered on money and production for their own sake.[67] These new processes are being led very authentically by the social and popular movements that struggle for the "active participation of great majorities."[68] Just as for John XXIII, in *Pacem in Terris*, these processes included those promoting workers and women, decolonization, and peace between peoples, for Francis they are all those movements that, in the face of the current prevailing direction of globalization, denounce its consequences—that is, exclusion and inequality—while at the same time proposing a more humane world, an alternative to the current system. This is the mediating, sociopolitical role of the popular movements, of which the Church had lost sight during the so-called ecclesial winter before the arrival of Francis.

We can better understand this if we move away from the ecclesial mindset criticized by Aparecida, and accept that "the world has a specific secular dimension, which has its own consistency and relative autonomy" (*GS* 34; 36). The secular dimension finds expression within the common notions of civilization or culture. It is in this secular realm that the Spirit of God acts and is present, "not only in people of good will taken individually, but also in society and in history, peoples, cultures, religions."[69] To take on secular history with all its depth and truth means believing that the Spirit is present in it, in all these movements, forces, and processes in history, beyond the institutional Church, and that they bear in themselves a saving orientation greater than that which is immediate and palpable. Such a vision helps convert the Church, helps it to go out of itself and accompany these processes of humanization or "*growth in humanity* which draw us near to reproducing the image of the Son so that He may be the firstborn among many brethren" (*Medellín* 4, 9)— in other words, to work together toward achieving concrete expression of the universal brother/sisterhood of all peoples and their cultures.[70]

3

TOWARD A LIBERATING PASTORAL MINISTRY OF PEOPLES AND THEIR CULTURES

Turning toward persons and fostering their liberation

Evangelization is the great post-council issue,[1] one that results from a church beginning to understand more fully what it means to be people of God called to live in the midst of the other peoples of the earth (*LG* 17; *Ad Gentes* [*AG*] 5). This new vision was made possible thanks to what Karl Rahner called the anthropological turn precipitated by Vatican II, which Rafael Tello in Argentina interpreted as a return to concrete, real persons in history:

> Not toward the abstract human being, considered according to a certain idea or conception of what he or she is, nor viewed only according to his or her nature (which would still be abstract), but toward the concrete, real, historic, and individually existing human being, that is, the whole human being and each human being born of woman, created and called by God to participate in his life, which is eternal, and by that very fact the whole human being, in all his or

her dimensions—eternal and temporal, spiritual and corporal, individual and communal—*all* human beings and *each one* of them.[2]

The great merit of the council spirit, as Tello explains, was to have understood quite clearly that "the human being—in this life—is what matters, and what matters for all, universally, is to be able to improve living conditions in this world (progress, development)." The council had marked a new direction for the mission of the Church, the starting point of which was recognition of "the autonomy of human beings, society, and science (*GS* 36), of human culture (*GS* 59), and of the temporal order in general (*AA* 7)." It had affirmed that that autonomy is "aimed at the perfection of human beings and their life in God."[3] It had established that between God and the human being there is no contradiction or antagonism whatsoever, but rather reciprocity and empowerment of capabilities. This new direction involves acknowledging the transcendental and revelatory value of human praxis, for in it human beings manifest their totality, what they are and do in the world, their worldly existence. Indeed, this very way of being and dwelling of human beings, of existing, becomes site of revelation and encounter with God (*GS* 22).

Years later, Paul VI in *Evangelii Nuntiandi* (*EN*) explained the implications of this turn in terms of an evangelized and evangelizing Church, called to preach the Kingdom of God which has begun in this history (13–14). Pope John Paul II would later go on to state in *Redemptoris Missio* that the path of the Church is that of human beings, and its mission is that of helping to make "human life ever more human."[4] Indeed, although the liberation of human beings and peoples was not explicitly addressed at Vatican II (*GS* 53–62), it shed light on the horizon of the mission of the Church in this new era and its influence is evident in the papal documents that followed the council. The actual topic of liberation and of the option for the poor was to be the specific contribution of the Latin American Church to the universal Church. Only from a liberation rooted in an option for the poor can the anthropocentric individualism characteristic of modernity be overcome. Hence, the novelty of the council is to have turned its gaze to human beings as subjects, in themselves, beyond anything that they may do or have. As the Argentine theologian Omar César Albado explains:

> The Church turns toward concrete human beings not for what they can come to be (in terms of their social position or their education), but *simply because they are human beings*. The rest may come later, but it is not in any way a condition for deciding to give them attention. Their dignity does not depend on whether they can read or write, whether they have electricity or natural gas, but solely and simply because they are human beings created by God. This is how the anthropological turn differs from anthropocentrism.[5]

This turn was to shape a new paradigm of the Church's presence and action in history. The axiom "outside the church there is no salvation," has given way to another one that is more inclusive and truly catholic (universal) namely, "outside humankind there is no salvation." The movement is from believing that only a few can be saved provided they belong to the church institution and adapt to it, to declaring that all of us, living in kinship and solidarity, especially with the poor, are saved because we are on the same path of history. It is a move from a doctrinaire attitude that posits a conception of absolute truth as the source of all rights to a position that appreciates and promotes the exercise of one's own conscience as an expression of human dignity, even when acting erroneously (cf. *DH* [*Dignitatis Humanae*] 2). This turn leads to holding that any action of the Church ought to be liberating, ought to humanize human relations and repair structures. Every Church action must have a real effect on the actual life of persons and their social relations.

A Latin American option: From Medellín to San Miguel

The relationship between theology and liberation was first mentioned at a gathering of theologians at the Franciscan Theological Institute in Petrópolis, Brazil, in 1964. There an effort was made to analyze the situation of the Latin American Church in light of the winds of change that had begun to be felt in the years of the council. Among the participants were Gustavo Gutiérrez, Juan Luis Segundo, and Lucio Gera, who spoke about the function of theology and the role of the theologian. Four years later, at the 1968 Gathering of Priests and Laypeople organized by the ONIS (National Office of Information) priest movement in Chimbote, Peru, Gutiérrez gave a talk entitled, "Toward a Theology of Liberation." The theological reflection emerging in Latin America was thus given a name.

During those years, various gatherings for reflection on evangelization and social ministry were also taking place. Three were organized in 1965 by the Latin American Pastoral Institute (IPLA) under CELAM, directed by the Chilean theologian Segundo Galilea, and held in Bogotá, Havana, and Cuernavaca. Other gatherings took place in

Santiago, Chile, and in Montevideo, Uruguay (1967). Formal consolidation of liberation language and the assumption
of the people as subject in the Church took place specifically
at the second meeting of the Conference of Latin American
Bishops (CELAM II) in Medellín (1968).

The *Medellín Document* expressed the reception of
Gaudium et Spes in Latin America. However, assessment of it
cannot be limited to a particular time and place, applicable
only to the Church in Latin America. The document presents a critical vision of the global structures affecting human
development, especially that of the poor, structures that as-
sault the integrity of peoples and their cultures. Thus, the
critique of *Medellín* is against an existing "structure of sin"
that does not allow for creating conditions of a decent life for
all, but only for a few. It takes a stance against systems that
make use of the human being and absolutize their own ideological positions. Hence the accusation is that:

> the system of liberal capitalism and the temptation of
> the Marxist system would appear to exhaust the pos-
> sibilities for transforming the economic structures of
> our continent. Both systems militate against the dig-
> nity of the human person. One takes for granted the
> primacy of capital, its power and its discriminatory
> utilization in the function of profit-making. The
> other, although it ideologically supports a kind of hu-
> manism, is more concerned with collective humanity
> and in practice becomes a totalitarian concentration
> of state power. We must denounce the fact that Latin
> America sees itself caught between these two options
> and remains dependent on one or other of the cen-
> ters of power that control its economy.[6]

In no way taking ideological stances, *Medellín* makes a holistic proposal for liberation and comprehensive development of the human being, which calls for integration and collaboration between individuals, groups, and intermediate associations and members of the economic and political sectors. It is assumed that those most affected by the current situation are to take part in decision-making about their future, and not be limited to being treated as objects by big-money interests. To that end the bishops urge the personalization of sociopolitical processes and structures at every level, adding that "the necessary changes [need to] take place from within, that is to say, from a fitting awakening of conscience, adequate preparation, and the effective participation of all, which ignorance and the often inhuman conditions of life make it impossible to assure at this time."[7]

It thus begins to be understood that setting in motion sociopolitical processes for the sake of the common good is part of the church institution's task of evangelization, of its process of insertion into and humanization of peoples and their cultures, insofar as they represent group, not individual, ways of life with a just "aspiration for their liberation and growth in humanity."[8] The response of the Church to injustice is inspired not by a political design but by the Church's mission to "defend the rights of the poor and oppressed according to the gospel commandment, urging our governments and upper classes to eliminate anything that might destroy social peace: injustice, inertia, venality, insensitivity."[9]

The great ecclesial contribution of CELAM II in Medellín is that it explained that the Church must assume its historical responsibility, but as subject, with its own voice in society and with a meaningful proposal. It must be a church that treats others as agents with shared responsibility, seeing the *locus* of the people's situation as a place for God's revelation; a church that understands itself not only as bearing and leading the poor, but also as being borne and evangelized by them. The most appropriate action for the Church will be not revolutionary or political but social, rooted in discernment of the contemporary signs of the time as authentic theological *loci* from which God challenges us and before which we cannot remain indifferent. Such a stance derives from the Church's evangelizing practice, its missionary dimension, and its activity aimed at unleashing processes of evangelization that take into account these new signs of the times. Hence

> evangelization must direct itself toward the formation of a personal, internalized, mature faith that is operative and constantly confronting the challenges of present-day living in this era of transition. Evangelization needs to be in harmony with the "signs of the times." It cannot be outside time and history. In fact, the "signs of the times," which on our continent are expressed above all else in the social order, constitute a "theological locus" and a mandate from God.[10]

In light of the change of era and the application of new theological methods of discernment, Medellín played a decisive role in forming the consciousness and identity of the Church in Latin America. The attempt was made to move toward a Church that would cease to be European and would begin to have its own characteristics "based on and for its peoples and their cultures";[11] a Church that would understand the communal dimension of the faith and evangelizing action as proper to its mission and identity, rejecting the temptation to isolate itself in private religion and devotional practices.[12] Archbishop Eduardo Pironio of Ecuador describes Medellín as a saving event that began a new period for the Church in Latin America, that called it to become converted to the poor and serve them.[13]

Christian faith is thus presented in a new way, as the horizon of an effort to build a brother/sisterly life by gathering in small communities of shared life and communion. This allows for the formation of social bonds of brother/sisterhood based on experiences similar to those of the earliest Christian gatherings. The proposed style, grounded in the creation of base communities—not parish groups—combines spirituality, evangelization, and human development as symbolic and interpersonal embodiments of the Kingdom unfolding in history. One of the richest texts along these lines reads:

> The Christian ought to find the living out of communion, to which he has been called, in his "base community,"...whose size allows for personal fraternal contact among its members. Consequently, the Church's pastoral efforts must be oriented toward the transformation of these communities into a "family of God," beginning by making itself present among them as leaven, as a nucleus, although it be small, that creates a community of faith, hope, and charity. Thus the Christian base community is the first and fundamental ecclesiastical nucleus, which on its own level must make itself responsible for the richness and expansion of the faith, as well as for worship, which is the expression of faith. This community thus becomes the initial cell of ecclesiastical structure and the focus of evangelization, and it serves as the most important factor in the promotion of human advancement and development.[14]

Another element contributing to this perspective of liberation and integral development was COEPAL's theology of the people or of culture and the theological thought of the Argentine theologian Lucio Gera. The terms "liberation" and "transformation of structures" were a consistent part of the language used by members of the commission and are found in the *San Miguel Document*. In the chapter dealing with justice, the mediations for bringing about this liberating action are explained:

> Since the supreme vocation of human beings is only one and divine, the mission of the Church is also one: to save human beings in the entirety of their humanity. Hence, evangelization necessarily encompasses the entire realm of human experience. Thus it is our duty to work for the complete liberation of human beings and to shed light on the process of changing the unjust and oppressive structures produced by sin. Liberation must accordingly take place in all realms where there is oppression: legal, political, cultural, economic, and social.[15]

New realms of pastoral involvement appear, such as the legal, political, economic, and social realms, thereby leading to the need to think through new challenges and modes for engaging in evangelization. The proclamation of the Gospel can no longer be understood in isolation from the local culture in all its complexity, because, as Gera explained, culture is "the life of peoples and human beings,"[16] and evangelizing means being inserted into "the set of evaluative experiences—and of evaluative absences—proper to and characteristic of a people."[17] Any action of evangelization will entail a process that leads to the transformation and liberation of persons and structures from within, from the sociocultural mediations in which persons live and conduct their lives in society (*Puebla* 392). Engaging in these mediations will make it possible to move "from less human to more human conditions."[18]

The *San Miguel Document* recognizes the people's culture as the ethico-mythic core that must be preserved, and it asserts that people need to be freed from any outside influence that would change them through ideology. To understand the popular realm means to understand the community matrix of the experience of faith. As Rafael Tello has said, "In order to be oriented to God, popular culture looks at concrete human beings who, being social, exist in a community, that is, in a people, which as a whole lives among earthly realities. That is their world."[19] Thus the popular realm is the site of liberating or prophetic ministry, insofar as this means responding to the signs of the times as evidenced in the sociocultural reality of poor peoples, who constitute the majority of humankind.

Popular pastoral ministry has helped overcome an ecclesial culture that represents an image of God over and against the world. The people's culture does not reflect the scheme of formal religion; it is based on the relationship with a God who is manifested in and through the everyday life of each person, whether in the realm of the outward and secular or of the silent and symbolic-mythical. Among the people there is a true encounter between faith and culture; it is an everyday personalized faith, rather than one that is private and turned inward. This is the context for understanding the proposal of the *San Miguel Document* for a church for the poor which "discerns reality from the perspective of the people and their interests" and which recognizes the people, in keeping with Medellín, as "subject and agent of history"[20] rather than as an object of sociopolitical or religious indoctrination.

Thus, according to the *Medellín Document*, "the Church in Latin America should be manifested, in an increasingly clear manner, as truly poor, missionary and paschal, separate from all temporal power and courageously committed to the liberation of each and every man;"[21] or, in other words, "a Church of the poor in fidelity to their being sacrament of Christ."[22] These ecclesiological and Christological perspectives would be foundational for Francis from the outset of his papacy as keys to approaching the process of reform. The contribution arising from ecclesial life and theological reflection in Latin America can be seen in terms of the Church having made a radical, and therefore constitutive, shift in understanding its relationship with the poor and their cultures. As Pedro Trigo describes it:

> What is crucial is that one live the relationship as a process in which one reaches a moment when it is possible to say that one not only "takes on" and "bears" the problems and potentialities of the people, to the point of "bearing with them," but also that one "feels borne by them," receives grace from them and through them. At this point, one becomes another person, a true brother or sister in Christ. At that moment, the act of giving does not humiliate the receiver, because the receiver is also the one who gives. One is, in reality, of the people, as the people are of oneself.[23]

From the synods of bishops to Evangelii Nuntiandi

Following on the stimulus provided by Medellín, the relationship between evangelization, justice, and liberation was acknowledged by the universal magisterium in the 1971 *Declaration of the Second General Assembly of the Synod of Bishops on Justice in the World*. In that declaration, the assumption is that the Church is called to respond to the new signs of the times as urged by *Gaudium et Spes*, "proclaiming the Good News to the poor, freedom to the oppressed, and joy to the afflicted."[24] The synod holds that the actions of preaching, liberating, and giving joy flow from the Church's Christological calling and not from a political option, that is, that they have to do with the "constitutive dimension of the preaching of the Gospel."[25] Fidelity to the Gospel entails "a call to people to turn away from sin to the love of the Father, universal kinship, and a consequent demand for justice in the world."[26]

Liberation is here used as a synonym of salvation and is presented in two contexts: (1) promotion of the human being, which leads to economic growth and sociopolitical participation;[27] and (2) the development of peoples themselves to free themselves from any form of colonialism. In both cases, the synod was continuing the theme opened by Medellín.

Nevertheless, the issue of liberation was taken up yet again, on its own terms, by the Third General Synod of Bishops on Evangelization of the Contemporary World, held in 1974.[28] At that synod, the bishops of the entire world discussed liberation as a proper function of the Church's labor of evangelization in each culture. Archbishop Eduardo Pironio, in his presentation, spoke of the need for a new evangelization based on three pillars: (1) proclamation of the praxis of Jesus, (2) proclamation of the transforming power of the Reign, and (3) the call to conversion of the Church. This type of liberation is an action of *diakonia* of the entire people of God, the fruit of which is salvation.[29]

Evangelization is not a matter of teaching previously developed, self-enclosed doctrines unrelated to the reality of the people living in a particular culture. For Archbishop Pironio, any action of evangelization will be meaningful if it responds to the signs of the times, because "evangelization is directly related to the promotion of human development and the full liberation of peoples, without thereby entailing the idea that the Reign of God and human development are identical."[30]

These ideas situate evangelization within the very dynamism of the humanizing processes of societies through their historic, social, economic, political, and religious mediations. The proclamation of the good news of Jesus always has a character of *eu-topía*—(a joy experienced here and now)—not utopia (an expectation of a future place of wellbeing)—because it should impel us toward supporting what leads to joy, everything good (such as justice, brother/sisterly relations, and hope), for which there must be as much room as possible in this world. In other words, the proclamation of "the Gospel must be a concrete response to the legitimate aspirations of men and women and their communities."[31] Otherwise, the proclamation will be insignificant, irrelevant, because it will not have a prophetic character.

Again, this connection between evangelization processes and the proclamation of liberation of the human being goes hand in hand with what the bishops meeting in Medellín had sought: "the face of a Church that is truly poor, missionary and paschal, separate from all temporal power and courageously committed to the liberation of each and every man."[32] Indeed the 1974 synod of bishops placed the problem of the credibility of the Church in this context of a proclamation of the Gospel, as sociohistorical and cultural liberation, for "unless the Christian message of love and justice shows its effectiveness through action in the cause of justice in the world, it will only with difficulty gain credibility with the people of our time."[33]

The conclusions of the synod were incorporated by Paul VI into the formulation of the apostolic exhortation *Evangelii Nuntiandi* in 1975. In this document the pope states that "evangelization involves an explicit message, adapted to different situations...about the rights and duties of every human being, about family life without which personal growth and development is hardly possible, about life in society, about international life, peace, justice and development—a message, especially relevant in our day, about liberation."[34] This is a liberation applicable on three levels: anthropological (which begins by recognizing the concrete social and economic problems of each human subject), theological (inasmuch as there is no redemption without justice), and evangelical (because love for neighbor entails his or her growth in humanity).[35] Accordingly, the pope says, it cannot be accepted

> that in evangelization one could or should ignore the importance of the problems so much discussed today, concerning justice, liberation, development and peace in the world. This would be to forget the lesson that comes to us from the Gospel concerning love of our neighbor who is suffering and in need.[36]

Both at the 1974 synod of bishops and in *Evangelii Nuntiandi* (1975), Paul VI connects the word "liberation" with actions of social and human development that are carried out as part of the process of evangelization but lived in the context of a larger event that is salvific and that is taking place within this history, not outside of it. The process ultimately has to do with the establishment of the Kingdom of God, which, while already beginning in history, is not to be identified with temporal ideological systems, which would reduce it to a mere immanent reality.[37] Nevertheless, the exhortation, following the spirit of the council, makes it clear that there is no salvation without full liberation from everything that oppresses the human and prevents human beings from developing;[38] to opt for any other approach "would be to ignore the teaching of the Gospel about love for the neighbor who suffers or endures need."[39]

The path of Puebla and Bergoglio's contribution

A few years later, the CELAM III meeting in Puebla (1979) took up the new approach that had arisen in Latin American theology and had been incorporated into Paul VI's *Evangelii Nuntiandi*. Puebla reexamined in depth the historical and sociocultural context of Latin America, presenting chapters on "Evangelization of Culture" (*Puebla* 385–443), "Evangelization and Popular Religiosity" (*Puebla* 444–469), and "Preferential Option for the Poor" (*Puebla* 1134–1165). In them, under the inspiration of—and in some cases written directly by—Lucio Gera, the theme of culture is addressed and dealt with as an ethical and religious reality that requires a "liberating evangelization" (*Puebla* 485, 487, 488, 489).

The *Puebla Final Document* states that the aim of the "doctrine of the Church is always the promotion and development of human beings in terms of both their earthly and their transcendent dimensions. It is a contribution to the construction of the ultimate and definitive Kingdom" (*Puebla* 475). It further specifies that "this liberation is gradually being realized in history, in our personal history and that of our peoples. It takes in all the different dimensions of life: the social, the political, the economic, the cultural, and all their interrelationships. Through all these dimensions must flow the transforming treasure of the Gospel" (*Puebla* 483). Francis would say the same thing in 2013 in words that we have previously quoted and that are worth recalling: "No one is saved by himself or herself, individually, or by his or her own efforts. God attracts us by taking into account the complex interweaving of personal relationships entailed in the life of a human community."[40] This is the human realm formed by the "set of relationships" in which we develop and are saved.

The *Puebla Final Document* echoes the thought of Gera, for whom history unfolds through processes in which the religious and the secular are united under the impetus toward liberation as authentic sign of God in the midst of his people.[41] Thus, with the expression "evangelization of culture," acts of evangelization are constitutively bound to liberating activities—and therefore to the relational and social order—so that "it is no longer a matter of the Church's social ministry, but it is simply pastoral ministry or evangelization, which includes, as an integral part, the social dimension or advancement of the human in terms of development and liberation (cf. *Puebla* 355). This maintains firmly as foundation, center, and culmination or essential content the salvation that Jesus Christ, Son of God made to humanity and offers to all human beings as a gift of grace and of God's mercy (cf. *Puebla* 351)."[42]

The Puebla focus started from the premise that "new situations that arise from sociocultural changes call for a new evangelization" (*Puebla* 366). Puebla's intuition of a new era calling for a new evangelization[43] was taken up by John Paul II, who in Haiti, in his 1983 speech before the preparatory assembly for the Fifth Centenary of the Evangelization of America, enshrined Puebla's formula of new evangelization, referred to "a commitment by you the bishops, together with your priests and people, a commitment not to a re-evangelization but to a new evangelization—new in ardor, methods, and expression."[44] We see here an important change not only of accent but even of perspective. What does this mean?

Puebla had regarded evangelization as a process of entering into the various sociocultural spaces of society in light of the challenges posed by the change of era announced in *Gaudium et Spes* and reaffirmed in Medellín. Hence, the challenge was in thinking through the new realms of sociopastoral action. However, the post-synod exhortation *Ecclesia in America* promulgated by John Paul II in 1997 (*On the Encounter with the Living Jesus Christ: The Way to Conversion, Communion and Solidarity in America*), would represent a significant reversal. In this document evangelization is no longer understood as being in tune with sociohistorical processes of transformation, nor is primacy given to sociocultural involvement. What is presented is the need to find new methods and ways of having the message (kerygma) reach people, with the aim of recovering those spaces lost to the Church in a world that is steadily withdrawing from the contents of the faith and from a moral appraisal of reality.[45]

The proposal focused on three basic reference points or places for encounter with Christ: scripture, interpreted according to church tradition; the liturgy, centered on the Eucharist; and commitment to the poor.[46] However, the document defines the poor as the addressees and recipients of a preferential "social and charitable work,"[47] not as subjects of a process of evangelization and liberation in history. In dealing with the poor it goes no further than making a pastoral appeal in two directions: to alleviate the most serious and urgent needs of the poor, and to denounce the roots of the evil that spring from social, political, and economic structures.[48]

What this meant was that greater emphasis was now being placed on individual conversion along the lines of the "Christendom" model. No connection was made between the forms of ecclesial structure and the crisis in the transmission of the faith, nor was evangelization seen as having anything to do with the processes of sociopolitical transformation of peoples. One could speak of pastoral ministry being reduced to a focus on the search—quasi-technical and with a view to teaching doctrine—for new methods and ways of approaching society. It is true that *Ecclesia in America* spoke of the negative effects of neoliberal globalization because of the growing and narrowly economic view of human beings. However, the document did not address the essential bond—recognized as a result of reflection on the part of the magisterium and insights arising from Latin American theologies—between evangelization and actions on behalf of liberation and social development, a bond that is an expression of intense Christian life lived out in keeping with the signs of the times. With Rafael Tello, we could say that there was a tilt toward a focus on "ecclesial culture," with the accent on giving aid with little focus on the person, leaving aside the universal particularity of the people's culture, which had been one of the great achievements of Latin American church life and theology, and whose starting point was a Christian ethic of solidarity and what Puebla called "solidary forms of social life" (*Puebla* 414).

A process of regression like this happens when real connections with the agency of the people is lost, when we write without even having had dealings with those about whom we are writing, when we have no knowledge of specific processes and ways of formalizing reality in popular cultures. In other words,

> the greatest obstacle [here] is educated elite identity: one assumes that one lives a life so qualitatively superior to that of the people that one can only give one's

own treasure so that the other may become as enriched as oneself. In saying 'one' we are not referring to the individual that one is, but rather to the cultural and social identity, assumed personally. From this perspective there is no room for mutual relationship; it will always be one-way. Giving is generally done with humility, with kindness, even with respect. But it is one's own self who has something to give, because the paradigm of humanity is oneself, not the people. Anyone who does not radically and concretely relativize his or her own paradigm of humanity cannot receive anything important from the people.[49]

In the midst of all the debates and proposals after Puebla, it is important to recall that, in 1985 while he was rector of the Colegio Máximo, the then father Bergoglio organized a conference under the title: Congress on the Evangelization of Culture and Inculturation of the Gospel. It was the first time in Latin America that a conference had been devoted solely to reflection on the inculturation of the Gospel. Cardinal Paul Poupard and many Latin American bishops were among those who attended. Bergoglio gave the opening address, in which he emphasized how important it is that we approach the life-world of the people in order to be able to generate processes of evangelization that will give momentum to social changes. He quoted Father Pedro Arrupe, SJ, superior general of the Jesuits and a pioneer in the use of the neologism "inculturation." According to Arrupe, "inculturation is the incarnation of the Christian life and Christian message in a specific cultural context, in such a way that this experience not only finds expression through elements proper to the culture in question (this alone would be no more than a superficial adaptation), but becomes a principle that animates, directs and unifies the culture, transforming and remaking it so as to bring about a new creation."[50]

This way of connecting with the cultural situation of the people through processes of inculturation of the Gospel had been central to the Argentine theology of the people in the late 1960s. Drawing inspiration from this theological and ecclesial context, and supported by the findings of the discernment effort led by Father Arrupe on the universal mission of the Society of Jesus in the 1970s, Father Bergoglio believed that the option for the poor necessarily involves knowledge of their cultures. This is because, as he stated in his opening remarks to the 1985 Congress on the Evangelization of Culture and Inculturation of the Gospel, "just as Christ, incarnate Wisdom, is the sole mediator between God and human beings, it could be said that the cultures of peoples, as wisdom, are a privileged space of mediation between the Gospel and human beings, as is evident in the results of our collective work throughout history." Any process of inculturation is therefore *intra societatem* and precedes the proclamation of the kerygma.

Bergoglio makes his own the call made by Arrupe in his "Letter on Inculturation" and working document sent to all members of the Society of Jesus in 1978. The letter states that "if inculturation is something experiential, it is clear that it also entails identification with the sufferings of a people and with their yearnings for liberation and growth in authentic values. Thus, inculturation requires that all of us work directly or indirectly for the poor and from the poor, in the sense that evangelization must be done from the perspective of the poor of Yahweh, of poverty of spirit, which prepares us to receive Christ. Inculturation and the promotion of justice entail one another."[51]

The novel aspect of Bergoglio's presentation lay in granting primacy to "inculturation of the Gospel" rather than to the "evangelization of culture"—a primacy that highlights the importance of preservation of the culture and its liberation from any attempt at outside cultural domination.[52] A new accent is thus placed on the manner of being Church *in actu*, for it implies that the local church must first know and assume the sociocultural reality in which it lives and is expressed, and in this manner connect with the poor peoples whom it must serve in fidelity to its following of Jesus.

The proclamation of the Gospel is not abstract nor is it done from the outside; it is concrete and is proclaimed from within, along with peoples and with them. Evangelizing does not mean imposing a Christian culture,[53] let alone an ecclesial culture; it does not mean stripping a culture of its original identity, but making accessible the message of Jesus and learning to respond in accordance with the requirements of each people and of each age without falling into a form of trivial adaptation that ultimately extinguishes gospel prophecy.[54] It becomes a principle that animates, directs, and unifies the culture, transforming and remaking it so as to bring about "a new creation." Evangelizing means looking at the world from the life of peoples, respecting their many cultures and being integrated into them and, within each culture, paying special attention to religiosity as the privileged hermeneutic location for getting to know how poor peoples think and live. Certainly this implies a cultural shock for anyone who becomes inculturated, as Father Arrupe explains:

> If [we] want to let ourselves be caught up in the process of inculturation, theory and study are not enough. We need the shock of a deep personal experience. For those called to live in another culture, it will mean being integrated into a new country, a new language, a whole new life. For those who remain in

their own country, it will mean experiencing the new
styles of our changing contemporary world—not the
mere theoretical knowledge of the new mentalities,
but the experiential assimilation of the way of life of
the groups with which we must work, the outcasts,
Chicanos, slum dwellers, intellectuals, students,
artists, etc.[55]

This vision is fully in accord with Vatican II, for it holds
that the religious mission of the Church (*GS* 42) consists in
helping to discover and energize the transcendence of the
human (*GS* 11). This is the "new humanism" about which
Paul VI spoke in *Populorum Progressio* (16, 20, 42), which must
be "global" (72). Hence, the work of evangelization can no
longer be understood apart from its connection to promoting
processes of humanization that build "a new humanism, one
in which people are defined first of all by this responsibility to
their brothers and sisters and to history" (*GS* 55).

Analysis of the processes of inculturation of the Gospel
thus led to a rethinking of the identity of the Church in relation to its mission. This is because these processes affect the
way of entering into sociocultural situations as well as the
perspective that emerges as a result of living within them.
Likewise, the new contexts and cultural situations in which
the Church was becoming involved at the time presented
corresponding challenges that had to be met. The processes
of insertion into the life-worlds of poor peoples made it possible to see situations from within, from the perspective of
the victims and of those suffering from the sociocultural
processes of transformation driven by the global age of technology, secularism, and interculturality. Some theologians
came to understand that "the Church does not have a mission, but rather the mission has a Church,"[56] for the primary

thing is its *discipleship identity*, which places it in the *state of continually going out of itself* to encounter the other from within and on the basis of his or her life-world. This outgoing movement draws inspiration from the historical praxis of Jesus, who always went out to meet the other, the needy, and marginalized, and it was these encounters with persons in concrete situations that changed his life.

New developments at Aparecida

The Fifth General Conference of the Bishops of Latin America and the Caribbean Bishops, or CELAM V, was held at the sanctuary of Aparecida, Brazil, in 2007, the high point of globalization. Bergoglio played a decisive role as head of the drafting committee of the final document. The emphasis in that document is not placed on going to mission sites where the first proclamation has not yet taken place, nor is it placed on renewal of parishes and sacramental structures in those places where faith and participation in the liturgy has been lost. Rather, the document insists on the importance of reaching the inhabitants of urban centers and their outskirts, both believers and non-believers.[57] The accent is those living on the peripheries, that is, on those who, regardless of their religious profession or political identity, are victims of exclusion as a result of the process of globalization. It is their reality as human beings, and all that they suffer, that the Church must assume as the new preferential social location.[58]

Today it is not enough to devise new pastoral methods, or update the language of doctrine, or improve mechanisms for charitable social action. What we are facing "is no longer simply the phenomenon of exploitation and oppression, but something new: social exclusion. What is affected is the very root of belonging to the society in which one lives, because one is no longer on the bottom, on the margins, or powerless, but rather one is living outside. The excluded are not simply 'exploited' but 'surplus' and 'disposable.'"[59] This text was quoted in *Evangelii Gaudium* (*EG* 53). A new pastoral challenge is posed, the recovery of the sense of belonging to society, to one's own culture, because the consequences of not doing so affect the very achievement of the vocation and identity of persons and peoples.

The global situation thus poses a new challenge to the ecclesial community: to rethink its sociocultural location from the peripheries,[60] because it is from there that the Church may again become a credible sign—there, where the excluded of all kinds, including those who are ecclesiastically excluded, are to be found. In order that this may happen, and in continuity with the magisterium and Latin American theology, CELAM V holds that evangelization processes must incorporate three essential elements: (1) the preferential option for the poor, (2) comprehensive human advancement, and (3) authentic Christian liberation.[61] The impetus for a new evangelization cannot be the recovery of what has been lost, but must be the generation of sociocultural processes for transformation, because "any evangelization process entails human advancement and authentic liberation, without which a just order in society is not possible."[62]

Aparecida echoes the message of Paul VI in Bogotá, where he said to the peasants: "You are a sign, a likeness, a mystery of Christ's presence" and then immediately proposed a most beautiful analogy: "The sacrament of the Eucharist offers us his hidden presence, living and real; you too are a sacrament, that is, a holy image of the Lord in the world, a reflection that is a representation and does not hide his human and divine face."[63] In light of that model, there is no room for religious or pastoral schemes that promote the privatization of religion or a Christianity without the Gospel, one that reduces faith to mere devotional or charitable acts or simply to formal participation in the eucharistic liturgy.

But this path is not easy, given the prevailing widespread tendency to promote an ecclesial culture that puts aside the centrality of personal encounter with Jesus and a reading of the gospels. There must be an "ongoing pastoral conversion"[64] of the "ecclesial structure" and its "way of relating" to society,[65] a structure which, after various crises, has lost the strength and glow of its credibility. The first step for bringing about this change "requires moving from a pastoral ministry of mere conservation to a decidedly missionary pastoral ministry,"[66] inspired by Vatican II. This means "making everything subject to establishing the Kingdom of God," and learning to "read the signs of the times."[67] Otherwise, we will have an insignificant church structure, one that is unattractive and cannot communicate the good news.[68]

The experience of pastoral conversion should situate ecclesial experience not only in a church "going out," but primarily as an *ecclesia semper reformanda* (*LG* 8), which must reject any self-referentiality and let itself be evangelized by the poor. That means being a church that can no longer understand its relationship with the world solely from the standpoint of what it offers sacramentally. This church is, above all, people of God set in the midst of the peoples and problems of this world (*EN* 15), and hence what it offers ought to draw inspiration from the following: (1) promoting personal encounter with Jesus; (2) situating the experience of faith in a community, rather than in an individualistic or private framework; (3) centering formation on the word of God, rather than on abstract ideas; and (4) recovering its missionary identity of going out to the other.[69]

One place where this pastoral conversion takes place is in the recognition that people's religious experiences are an authentic place of encounter with God—a subject that would later be taken up by Francis. People's religious experiences are not ritual expressions parallel to the official ones. They express a mystique[70] that is manifested in its own manner through the experience of "patron saint celebrations, novenas, rosaries, the Way of the Cross, processions, dances and songs of religious folklore, affection for the saints."[71] It is especially an experience of interior pilgrimage, one in which "the wisdom of love does not depend directly on the enlightenment of the mind, but on the internal action of grace."[72] The *Aparecida Docume*nt describes it in the following terms:

> The pilgrim's gaze rests on an image that symbolizes God's affection and closeness. Love pauses, contemplates mystery, and enjoys it in silence. It is also moved, pouring out the full load of its pain and its dreams. The confident prayer, flowing sincerely, is the best expression of a heart that has relinquished self-sufficiency, recognizing that alone it can do nothing. A living spiritual experience is compressed into a brief moment.[73]

This experience is based on a *communal model* that intrinsically relates faith to people's everyday life. It is rooted in people's way of being, and so makes it possible to overcome elitist or closed visions that can exist in church ministry and to resist attempts at ideological manipulation of religious phenomena.[74] Popular religion or Catholicism does not derive from a populist activity or a practice of the masses. It is more than anything else a religion concerned with re-connection [*religación*], one in which openness to the gift of God is recognized as the primary act and experience. The journey through life is not made alone. Through religious practices, deeply rooted human values and ways of integrating faith with local cultures are shared. These practices reveal a sense of faith that is an alternative to the growing tendency to privatize religion, with the ensuing loss of sociocultural rootedness, religious belonging, and community integration.

Popular religion has the great value—and in this is its most radical contribution to our globalized age—of recovering the transcendent meaning of shared everyday life. The everyday is not merely doing things every day, or being involved in the things that happen every day. It is an elemental experience that imparts agency, that enables us to integrate the things and actions that comprise the fabric of our lives without being consumed by despair and the exhaustion that can paralyze us and rob us of our future. It takes place when faith and daily life are symbiotically integrated, turning work into shared experience, the unexpected into gift, one's own need into openness to the other, and weariness into celebration and communal sharing. It is here that life encounters transcendence.

The new bishop of Rome:
"Living our human life to the fullest"

The CELAM general conferences in Río de Janeiro (1955), Medellín (1968), Puebla (1979), and Santo Domingo (1992) created spaces of communion and discernment shared by the different local churches in the face of the signs proper to each moment in time. Through these meetings, common directions for ecclesial style and pastoral praxis were able to be set. The meetings of the general conferences were unique to

Latin America. It is only recently, since the end of the twentieth century, that the churches on other continents have begun to engage in continent-wide synods similar to those of the Latin American church. These other synods, however, have not had a subsequent influence comparable to that of the Latin American conferences.

The CELAM general conferences had great influence on Jorge Bergoglio, and without an understanding of them we cannot have insight into the theological and pastoral perspective of Pope Francis or his vision for the universal Church. The conferences took place in the midst of continuous sociopolitical changes as well as economic and financial crises. Discussions at the conferences raised serious questions about the sociocultural locus of each people from within which the Church should situate itself and its relationship to the processes of evangelization; they also rejected the standardizing logic of cultural globalization.[75] In 2012, a year before being elected pope, Bergoglio insisted on the importance of this. Together with the Argentine bishops, he stated that "the rupture between the gospel and the culture, as Paul VI said, remains a challenge to which we must give priority. Personal encounter with Jesus Christ has to lead us to transform through the power of the Gospel our criteria for judgment, decisive values, points of interest, lines of thought, sources of inspiration, and models of life. The evangelization of culture is the sign of a mature faith that is taken on,"[76] because "culture, understood most broadly, represents the particular way that human beings and peoples cultivate their relationship with nature and with one another, with themselves and with God, so as to achieve a fully human existence."[77]

The election of Bergoglio as bishop of Rome opened a new channel for the theological and pastoral maturation of the vision of Church put forth in Latin America. The apostolic exhortation *Evangelii Gaudium*, published in 2013, cannot be understood apart from the influence of *Aparecida*. Thus, we agree with Carlos Galli when he says that "Bergoglio contributes with *Aparecida* and *Aparecida* contributes with Francis."[78] Nor may *Evangelii Gaudium* be understood without recognizing the relation between evangelization, the promotion of human development, and the liberation proposed in the magisterium of Paul VI. The importance of recognizing sociocultural location, as emphasized by the Argentine theology of the people and its reception in Puebla, is vital here. Bergoglio responds to the call made by Aparecida in 2007: "Let us recover our fervor of spirit. Let us preserve the wonderful and comforting joy of evangelizing, even when it is in tears that we must sow. May it mean for us ... an interior enthusiasm that nothing and nobody may quench. May it be the great joy of our consecrated lives ... the joy of Christ."[79] He repeats this text again in number 10 of *Evangelii Gaudium*. His words in Río of Janeiro in 2013 shed important light on the impact Aparecida has had on his vision for the Church: "The missionary discipleship which Aparecida proposed to the churches of Latin America and the Caribbean is the journey which God desires for the present "today.'"[80]

The apostolic exhortation *Evangelii Gaudium* calls for going to public spaces, the new agoras, for rejecting attempts at the privatization of religion, for moving away from devotional forms rooted in individualism and sentimentality (*EG* 70), and for overcoming a mentality of "charitable assistance" (*EG* 204). It is about recovering a Christianity with the Gospel (*EG* 11) in order to go out to encounter the peripheries (*EG* 20) with "new approaches and arguments on the issue of credibility" (*EG* 132). Ultimately, the idea is not to pursue the renewal of religion in order to make its practices more accessible and understandable to people today, but "to live our human life to the fullest" (*EG* 75), to rescue a religion with fraternal connection [*religación*]. This is where Christianity finds itself today, facing this vast horizon, this huge challenge, which for Francis translates into rebuilding social and economic bonds through kinship between persons and peoples. We find the basis of this focus in the call made by John XXIII,[81] followed by Vatican II[82] and by Paul VI, who summarizes it as follows:

> This duty concerns first and foremost the wealthier nations. Their obligations stem from the human and supernatural brotherhood of man, and present a three-fold obligation: (1) mutual solidarity—the aid that the richer nations must give to developing nations; (2) social justice—the rectification of trade relations between strong and weak nations; (3) universal charity—the effort to build a more humane world community, where all can give and receive, and where the progress of some is not bought at the expense of others. The matter is urgent, for on it depends the future of world civilization.[83]

Putting brother/sisterhood into practice leads to major pastoral consequences. It entails realizing that "the task of evangelization implies and demands the integral promotion of each human being" (*EG* 182), because I cannot be well while the other person, my kin, is doing badly. The struggle to improve the socioeconomic conditions of the other cannot remain a private or optional matter for some Christians or reserved to pastoral specialists for a few hours a week: it must flow forth from our need to live brother/sisterhood based on our following of Jesus.[84]

What is at stake is our fidelity to the Jesus of the Gospel, because "the kerygma—proclamation—has a clear social content" (*EG* 177). That this is not optional is clear "from the heart of the Gospel [where] we see the profound connection between evangelization and human advancement, which must necessarily find expression and develop in every work of evangelization" (*EG* 178). Here Francis is following the Jesuit Henri de Lubac, for whom "Catholicism is essentially social. It is social in the deepest sense of the word, not merely in its applications in the field of natural institutions but first and foremost in itself, in the heart of its mystery, in the essence of its dogma."[85] Thus, "each individual Christian and every community is called to be an instrument of God for the liberation and promotion of the poor, and for enabling them to be fully a part of society" (*EG* 187). Indeed, the issue is theological. The option for the poor is God's option, to which we respond as followers of Jesus: "Whatsoever you did for one of these least brothers of mine, you did for me" (Mt 25:40).

Thus, *the new evangelization* should include—inasmuch as the Church is the people of God among the peoples of this world—*those movements and social forces* that, even if not composed of Christians or believers, foster policies of inclusion out of a sense of justice and brother/sisterhood. They represent those who from the peripheries struggle for a better world despite having to go against the current. They live values that coincide with the praxis of Jesus of Nazareth, with the spirit of the Risen One. Encompassing "man's concrete life, both personal and social" (*EG* 181), these social movements also contribute to the evangelization of cultures and peoples, because "to evangelize is to make the kingdom of God present in our world" (*EG* 176). We are not speaking of a generic, abstract, uniform, homogenous-for-all world, but of each cultural realm in its concreteness. Francis's support for popular movements and social forces shows his commitment to fostering new alternative processes of change to make possible an improvement in the living conditions of those most in need. Here the duty of the Church is that of promoting and supporting engaged intellectuals who come from the people or who think from their perspective, whose work is not limited to the socioeconomic claims of the poorest sectors but includes recognizing and integrating the different ways of thinking and living that exist in today's multicultural world.

For Francis, the new evangelization, rather than emphasizing new methods and forms, is an invitation to bring in all those who struggle for the sociocultural recognition of the excluded, whose action springs from an authentic option for the poor as subjects—as opposed to being objects for receiving handouts—in a word, as people. As he notes, "It would be insufficient to envisage a plan of evangelization to be carried out by professionals while the rest of the faithful would simply be passive recipients. The new evangelization calls for personal involvement on the part of each of the baptized" (*EG* 120). This would have to be based on a theology of Christian life that goes beyond the prevailing clerical paradigm that puts the clergy above lay people. In light of the fact that that Jesus never lost his lay status, a Christian and ecclesial life that properly respects the relation between community and ministry must be based on the baptism of all the faithful rather than on the false dichotomy between men of God (priests) and people of the world (laity).[86]

Evangelizing is not a matter of regaining old lost spaces, or of fostering an ecclesial culture, but of giving space and voice to those who do not have them (*EG* 198),

to those excluded by political, economic, and religious systems, to those who live on the peripheries, for grace "is ac-
tivated and grows to the extent to which we go out to give
ourselves and to give the Gospel to others."[87] It is a matter,
then, of building bridges to bring about a better and more
human world. The entire effort of the Church toward a dialogue with the contemporary world must seek improvement in the living conditions of the majorities, and it must
press for "decisions, programs, mechanisms and processes
specifically geared to a better distribution of income, the
creation of sources of employment, and an integral promotion of the poor which goes beyond a simple welfare mentality" (*EG* 204). Here is where its fidelity to the Kingdom
of God is defined. In not doing these things, the Church
"would lose her fundamental meaning. Her message of liberation would no longer have any originality and would easily be open to monopolization and manipulation by
ideological systems and political parties."[88]

This social magisterium, whose core is the preferential
option for this majority, who are poor people, and which relates evangelization to the processes of human development
and liberation, is one of the great contributions of Latin
American theology, which began with the 1968 General
Conference of Latin American Bishops in Medellín. It
reaches us today through Francis, and thus actualizes in the
present the spirit of Vatican II. As the sign of a mature theology for these times of globalization and exclusion (*EG* 75),
it calls us to live our humanity deeply, not out of eccentric
or esoteric experiences, but from within cultures, in what is
most real and complex in social relations, in the very fabric
of personal relations. This is the only way in which a process
of transformation or conversion can come about.

Transforming cultures "from within"

Because he does not start from what Rafael Tello criticizes as the deep-seated tendency to form "ecclesial culture" rather than evangelical life, Francis believes, in keeping with the theology of the people, that every person is part of a people that is expressed in a particular sociocultural manner. It is in that people, and from within it, that every person is called to live his or her humanity. It is there that the Church must go and where evangelization must take place, rather than in the internal church realm, which would mean relapsing into self-referentiality. This aspect of Francis—which we have been discussing thus far, and which is embodied in the expression "Church going out"—has been the basis for his constant conviction and pastoral practice since his days in Argentina.

Francis has always believed—in accordance with the 1971 Synod of Bishops[89]—that processes of change and transformation should not be achieved by way of imposition or indoctrination. If that happens, we fall into new forms of colonialism. He explained this during his apostolic journey to Paraguay, where he warned that the Christian community "must be involved and incarnated in the national experience of the people and discern the liberating or saving action of the Church from the perspective of the people and their interests." Otherwise ideologies—or external cultural forms—will gain ground, and "ideologies end badly, and are useless. They relate to people in ways that are incomplete, unhealthy, or evil. Ideologies do not embrace a people."[90]

Francis upholds the sociocultural paradigm, because in it is still preserved the human interdependence that springs from the experience of shared daily life—something that gets lost in the fragmentation of hypermodernity. Here is how he understands the *sensus populi*, in the words of a talk given during his apostolic journey to Bolivia:

> This rootedness in the barrio, the land, the office, the labor union, *this ability to see yourselves in the faces of others*, *this daily proximity* to their share of troubles—because they exist and we all have them—and their little acts of heroism: this is what enables you to practice the commandment of love, not on the basis of ideas or concepts, but rather on the basis of *genuine interpersonal encounter*. We need to build up this culture of encounter. We do not love concepts or ideas; no one loves a concept or an idea. We love people.[91]

The vision of Francis leads to a change in the way we interact and situate ourselves socioculturally. Multicultural and pluricultural recognition that fails to put in practice *a sense of gospel interculturality* is insufficient. When we speak of multiculturality and pluriculturality we are concerned with each culture as different from the rest and, conscious of our own group and our own identity, we strive for respect and tolerance. The emphasis is on relations between groups and the need to achieve permanent bonds and points of encounter between them. Interculturality, on the other hand, is based on the praxis of encounter, cooperation, and interdependence, and hence it requires a pastoral style that is one-to-one, on a first-name basis, grounded in horizontal relationships that lead to mutual growth and the reciprocal exchange of gifts. In our age, in which a large portion of humankind lives out of a pragmatic and very localized immediate focus, snuffing out the innately human capacity to draw life from relationships, it is more than ever necessary—indeed urgent

—that an intercultural pastoral focus,[92] such as prevailed in the early days of Christianity, be recovered.

It is true that in novel or conflictive situations, one must begin by recognizing the diversity of cultures with an attitude of tolerance and respect and with the capacity to maintain one's own identity. That is the experience of migrants upon reaching a new culture. But the second step—perhaps the most important one for preserving one's own identity— is to foster participation in the sociocultural life of the welcoming country through interaction with completely different groups. This step must be taken by each person from his or her own way of being, without denying it or deprecating its value. It is not a matter of losing what is one's own and mixing it with something different, but of journeying together without sectarianism, of establishing kinship bonds and expanding the circle of our relationships. This demands of the Church—and of states as well—full recognition of the rights, responsibilities, opportunities, and duties of all those who live in a country, starting with genuine symmetrical relationships. It is in this sense that we have highlighted the importance of generating new processes of evangelization of peoples and their cultures.

What is noteworthy about this sociocultural approach is that it defends ways of life based on relationships of belonging and meaning. Recapitulating, we may say the following:

First, the word "culture" is used in two ways. In the singular, it refers to each person and in the plural it refers to peoples. As explained in the *Puebla Document*, "the term 'culture' refers to the specific way in which human beings belonging to a given people cultivate their relationship with nature, with each other, and with God (*GS* 53b) in order to arrive at 'an authentic and full humanity' (*GS* 53a). It is the style of common life (*GS* 53c) characterizing the various peoples; hence we speak about plurality of cultures (*GS* 53c)."[93]

Second, in the current multicultural framework, "only Christians from each culture will be able to implement the inculturation of Christianity in them."[94] Only thus will the temptation to smother the proper *ethos* of each by trying to impose an external ideology or value structure be averted.

Third, speaking of the evangelization of cultures does not mean adapting religious contents to each cultural group, but rather fostering processes of gospel-based consciousness-raising and human interaction of a symbolic horizontal nature that can favor a true reciprocity in dealing with the goods of civilization.

Hence, we must de-ideologize the interpretation of reality—political as well as religious—and recognize the urgent necessity of encountering one another, of fostering and accompanying the forces and movements that favor greater participation, integration, and interaction between the diverse groups living together in a single society. This is what Bergoglio saw in what was called "the faithful people," in what was a precursor to and paradigm for the culture and praxis of encounter that he proposed as an alternative to the current program of cultural and financial globalization. In his words:

> Out of readiness to serve, shaken by dire poverty and helplessness, torn by violence and drugs, bombarded by escapism of all kinds and shapes, we want to be reborn from our own contradictions. We accept the painful chalice, and we draw from our best reserves as people with little press and less advertising. In each individual and community effort of solidarity

emerging from a vast network of social organizations; in each researcher and scholar who strives for truth (although others relativize or go silent); in each educator and teacher who survives adversity; in each manufacturer who remains committed to labor; in each young person who studies, works, and makes a commitment by forming a new family; in the poorest and in all those who work or wearily seek work, who do not let themselves be dragged away by destructive marginalization or by the temptation to organized violence, but rather silently and with the strength to give of oneself made possible only by faith, keep loving their land. They have tasted a chalice, which in commitment and service has become balm and hope. In them is manifested the great cultural and moral reserve of our people. They are the ones who hear the word, those who bypass ritual applause, those who truly echo and understand that one does not speak for others.[95]

The *Aparecida Document* speaks of the new intercultural dynamic that has been taking shape in the global era, a dynamic that involves the mixing and sharing of new common spaces by a variety of urban and urban-periphery cultures of very different origins. This dynamic makes more urgent the need to formulate a theologico-pastoral model that will move in a new, symbiotic direction.[96] Pedro Trigo describes the challenge—which is essentially that of responding to the signs of the times in the contemporary age—in the following terms. It is a matter of "creating a multiethnic and pluricultural space characterized by justice, engagement, and solidarity in order to meet the challenge of shaping a polycentric and symbiotic form of globalization in which the fruits of the technological revolution can provide harmoniously for the good of all in a shared and sustainable manner."[97]

If we want evangelization to not be merely a process of religious indoctrination, as it has been in the past, then we must begin by recognizing the new sociocultural agents emerging in all their diversity, but within a framework of respect for the specificity of the ways of life of each of them. Evangelization takes place when the Gospel is inculturated in each of these ways of being, that is, when "it is inserted and incarnated in the national experience of the people and discernment is made of the Church's liberating salvific action from the perspective of each people and its interests."[98] *Evangelii Gaudium* describes this process of shared daily reality in moving terms: "An evangelizing community gets involved by word and deed in people's daily lives; it bridges distances, is willing to abase itself if necessary, and embraces human life, touching the suffering flesh of Christ in others. Evangelizers thus take on the 'smell of the sheep' and the sheep are willing to hear their voice" (*EG* 24).

Evangelizing action does not seek to restore the past or to idealize the present; to do otherwise would lead to trivial adaptations unable to attract anyone. Evangelizing processes are called to manifest their concern for people and to reject any imposition of a single globalizing model that would flatten all forms of life under a single parameter of being and acting, giving way to "homoginizing Westernization."[99] Such a model daily robs people of their inherent strength to link up with one another from what is deepest and most real in their existence.

The gaze of care for culture and history is one of the contributions of the Latin American Church that reaches us through the magisterium of Francis. We see reflected in it the insight of of Methol Ferré, one of the thinkers who has most influenced Bergoglio:

The evangelization process has been gradually embracing the many existing cultures; from its origins, the Church has had to establish dialogue with the most diverse cultures. Inasmuch as it must preach the Gospel to all nations, the question of the culture and cultures of human beings is consubstantial with the Church, and not abstractly, but in the changing heart of universal history, as a matter of life and death, of its reason for being.[100]

Years later Francis, following up on the insight of his dear friend Methol, would say that "each people is the creator of their own culture and the protagonist of their own history. Culture is a dynamic reality which a people constantly recreates; each generation passes on a whole series of ways of approaching different existential situations to the next generation, which must in turn reformulate it as it confronts its own challenges" (*EG* 122). The problem of peoples and their cultures is not an appendix to ecclesiology, let alone of pastoral theology. It is a vital and universal matter for Christian life, and therefore, consubstantial with the Church, with its identity and mission, wih its reason for being and its way of being in the world. Although the Church cannot be identified with any culture nor is it called to form Christian or ecclesial cultures, it must enter into cultures, care for their *ethos*, inasmuch as it is people of God in the midst of the peoples of the earth.[101]

4

PASTORAL GEOPOLITICS
OF PEOPLES AND THEIR CULTURES

Sources of a vision

On September 4, 2013, Pope Francis sent a letter to Russian president Vladimir Putin, who was presiding over the G20 leaders' summit in St. Petersburg. The letter contained a forceful message from the pope to those present at the meeting, heads of state with the largest economies on the planet, representing 90 percent of world GDP:

> The leaders of the G20 cannot remain indifferent to the dramatic situation of the beloved Syrian people, which has lasted far too long and risks bringing even greater suffering to a region bitterly tested by strife and in need of peace. To the leaders present, to each and every one, I make a heartfelt appeal to help find ways of dealing with the conflicting positions and to lay aside the futile pursuit of a military solution. Rather, let there be a renewed commitment to seek, with courage and determination, a peaceful solution through dialogue and negotiation of the parties, unanimously supported by the international community. Moreover, all governments have the moral duty

to do everything possible to ensure humanitarian assistance to those suffering because of the conflict, both within and beyond the country's borders.[1]

Three days after the meeting, in St. Peter's Square in Rome, Francis issued a powerful statement that included the refrain, "No more war!" Here the pope was taking his first geopolitical stand and beginning to give expression to a new Vatican diplomacy.[2] On various occasions since then, Francis has described the new geopolitical panorama as a World War III in stages,[3] which is being felt in various conflicts taking place in East Asia, North Africa, and the Middle East, as well as in the continual terrorist attacks that are affecting Europe and America. This age has brought into play new actors, of whom the diplomacy and geopolitical action of the Church must take note. In the words he used to address members of the Pontifical Academy of Social Sciences on April 18, 2015:

> Unfortunately, in a global economic system dominated by profit, new forms of slavery have developed, worse and more inhuman in a certain way, than those of the past... These new forms of slavery—human trafficking, forced labor, prostitution, organ trade— are extremely serious crimes, "an open wound on the body of contemporary society."[4]

But this is not just a simple denunciation. With each denunciation Francis sets in motion *processes* uniting persons, groups, institutions, and creeds on behalf of a common cause. A good example of this is the "Declaration of Religious Leaders against Slavery," a document resulting from extensive dialog and conversations among the leaders of the world's major religions and signed at the Pontifical Academy for Science in Rome in December 2014. In his address to participants, Pope Francis summed up their joint agreement on the evil of modern slavery: "The physical, economic, sexual and psychological exploitation of men, women and children that is currently inflicted on tens of millions of people constitutes a form of dehumanization and humiliation...Let us call to action all persons of faith and their leaders, governments, businesses, all men and women of good will to lend their unwavering support and to join the movement against modern slavery in all its forms."[5]

We live in a changing era, one that is no longer structured on the foundation of dual contending powers. Today there are many power centers, which, although sometimes diffuse and scarcely visible, can shift shape, even to the point of continually appearing and disappearing. We may speak of a *polycentric dynamic* that has come to take the form of a rejection—sometimes only by minorities—of attempts to centralize and restrict power to a few.

For Francis, the crisis of the age is driven by a globalizing model that originated in the Anglo-Saxon world and has become the new ideology of our time. We have seen Latin American theologians, the bishops in Aparecida, and then Francis himself in *Evangelii Gaudium* call it "capital fetishism" or "market totalitarianism" that makes money an absolute, a god, above human life itself. Specifically, Francis believes that it is the neoliberal proposal of contemporary capitalism that makes the market "the means, the method, and the goal that govern relationships among human beings,"[6] thereby relativizing the value of local cultures and their ways of life.

In 1964, Marshall McLuhan coined the term "global village." In 1968 the bishops at CELAM II in Medellín, following the line of thinking in Pius XI's encyclical *Quadragessimo anno*, spoke of the "imperialism of money," and in 1979 at CELAM III in Puebla spoke of the existence of a new "universal culture." However, it was in the 1990s, properly speaking, that these terms were linked to narrow economic neoliberal capitalism that imposes large corporations on local cultures without taking into account the people's own cultural values, and solely for the purpose of earning greater profit based on low labor costs.

This phenomenon was described in the *Letter and Study Document on Neoliberalism in Latin America of the Jesuit Provincials of Latin America* published in 1996, while Bergoglio was auxiliary bishop in Buenos Aires. In it is explained the process of globalization that "destroys the identity of local cultures that lack the ability to make themselves heard."[7] Work on this study document began in 1993 when the Jesuit province of Argentina asked that an interdisciplinary group be created to study neoliberalism in Latin America. The final version of the document was published in October 1996. The critique is not aimed at the globalization of the capitalist model in itself, but "against its neoliberal ideological interpretation." As Juan Carlos Scannone, SJ, observed, this interpretation "absolutizes and reduces the fact of globalization to its economic and financial aspects alone, which are true and important, but not the only ones. Moreover it reduces globalization to a single way of understanding it,"[8] and that is in terms of "complete liberalization, privatization, and deregulation."[9]

The negative effects of this model began to be felt geopolitically, in the sociocultural realm, as a result of the effects of mass media and technological innovations that have led to an ongoing standardization and homogenization of peoples and their cultures, their ways of living and of interacting. For Francis, this is the great problem of our age, against which his geopolitics is directed. The problem, however, is not in the form of a single model; rather, it is a way of operating and living that has become systemic and that kills. It kills ways of life, it steals the future, and it crushes hopes. In short, it relativizes the absolute value of cultures in order to sacralize the market and relationships of consumption. After many years the upshot has been that this prevailing tendency has become a system that denies "many millions of our brothers and sisters their most elementary economic, social, and cultural rights,"[10] because "man has been reduced to one of his needs alone: consumption."[11] Over against this situation there arises a challenge, the need to formulate a view that can permeate our geopolitical vision, relations between states, and relations with peoples and their cultures. The focus must be on creating processes that will make it possible to pass

> from an economy directed at revenue, profiting from speculation and lending at interest, to a social economy that invests in persons by creating jobs and providing training...We need to move from a liquid economy prepared to use corruption as a means of obtaining profits to a social economy that guarantees access to land and lodging through labor.[12]

This focus can be used to guide geopolitical discernment and pastoral actions and deeds, with the understanding that power ought to be at the service of the excluded and forgotten, those who are disregarded, those who are treated by the developed countries as though they do not exist—in other words, those whom large corporations use to increase production and who have to sacrifice their own lives, even running the risk of dying when they emigrate to other countries solely so that their children may have a future. The new focus, as we shall see, entails a change in the classic notion of geopolitics.

Old and new paradigms

The term "geopolitics" was coined by Rudolf Kjellen in 1899. In his work, *The State as Life Form,* he proposes that the state cannot be understood without its relationship to the geographical context—the *Lebensform* or life form—in which its inhabitants live. To explain this, he proposes three characteristics that delineate the relationships between geography and the politics of states or nations: (1) its position or *Topopolitik (Lage),* (2) its territoriality or *Physiopolitik (Raum),* and (3) its form or *Morphopolitik (Form).* Kjellen's theory serves to explain the need to occupy territories for the sake of the development of the inhabitants and the political projections of nations. Such was the case of General Karl Haushofer, who, in joining the Third Reich, insisted that political processes have to start from the occupation of territorial spaces that serve the purposes of expansion and development. Subsequent discourse, even to this day, would continue this paradigm of occupation, whether in the form of great empires, like that of Britain, that dominate entire nations; in the occupation of strategic spaces, as occurred during the Cold War era; or in the acquisition of environmental spaces, either for development or conservation. In all these examples the paradigm of occupation and expansion has driven the world political model.

Bergoglio's friend, the Uruguayan thinker Alberto Methol Ferré, was radically opposed to the colonizing and occupying tendency of geopolitics, whether by totalitarian states, neoliberal economics, or the imposition of a single global culture. Ferré's starting point is the fact that human beings are political by nature; that is how they position themselves toward reality. "The human being is an earthly and political animal, who naturally engages in 'geopolitics,' albeit in an elemental manner, not explicitly. Space is neutral only insofar as it is not dominated by the human being; it is only after being dominated that it is 'politicized.' Human struggles and conflicts always entail spatial conflicts and displacement."[13] This view, which would later influence the thought of Francis, focuses on culture as axial for discernment and geopolitical action. It is founded on recognition of the diversity of peoples inhabiting the world's geographical space, interacting among themselves from their many ways of living, mixing together to the point of forming a great *ecumene*.[14] However, this does not mean that one of these cultures has the right to impose itself politically, economically, or culturally on another. Rather, peoples are to forge their own destiny.[15]

In addition, an alternative geopolitical vision that overcomes the tendency toward uniformity must necessarily revise the relationship between political action and geographical reality through a *sociocultural*—as opposed to an ideological or narrowly economic—*model*. For Francis, such a model must be based on pursuit of the common good based on four criteria of discernment—or polarities in tension—that can serve to undergird the choice of journeys, words, and deeds: (1) "the whole before the part" (*EG* 234–236), (2) "reality before the idea" (*EG* 231–233), (3) "unity over conflict" (*EG* 217–237, *Lumen Fidei* [*LF*] 55.57), and (4) "time over space" (*EG* 217–237, *LF* 55.57). The interrelationship of these four principles gives shape to the Bergoglian image of the "polyhedron" as creative unity within diversity, where each—peoples and their cultures—contributes its own reality as part of the whole, and in which processes take place that over time will give life to new realities in the geographic space that they share.

In other words, this means that "we must live and build, keeping in mind the marvelous diversity of the world around us, avoiding the temptation to be fearful of others, of one who is unfamiliar to us, of one who does not belong to our ethnic group, to our political option, or to our religion. On the contrary, unity requires creating and fostering a synthesis of the wealth that each one bears within. Unity in diversity is a constant challenge that calls for creativity, generosity, self-sacrifice, and respect for others."[16] Such a synthesis is born of letting ourselves be touched by encounter with the other on a first-name basis—with no religious indoctrination, no barriers based on political ideologies—an encounter that leads to a new intercultural symbiosis. This means that Christianity cannot be identified with a single cultural mode, but that "it will also reflect the different faces of the cultures and peoples in which it is received and takes root."[17]

Putting in practice these criteria of discernment makes it possible to recalibrate the relationship between the whole— the fact of globalization—and the parts, the local cultures, with a broad long-range view and with open thinking that never shuts down or wearies of dialogue because *it doesn't regard anything as lost*. The point is to view actions as processes in time and not be in a hurry to occupy spaces. This latter approach is the characteristic of ideologies and religious indoctrination, but not of the Gospel—because "the fullness of time is not defined from a geopolitical perspective,"[18] which is only a new and important mediation in history.

The criteria help us discern the geopolitical realm, but in order for them to function in practice, and paraphrasing Lucio Gera, they demand a new mindset among diplomats.[19] This mindset must be animated by the goal of attaining universal kinship through what Francis calls the *utopia of the good* in order not to fall into sheer pragmatism, or into what is politically correct or simply philanthropic.[20] The pope expressed this new orientation of building bridges in his apostolic visit to the Central African Republic, when he addressed "the members of the diplomatic corps and the representatives of the international organizations, whose work recalls the ideal of solidarity and cooperation that needs to be cultivated between peoples and nations."[21]

We may deepen our understanding of the vision of Francis by considering certain ideas from the thought of philosophical theologian Erich Przywara, SJ, whom the pope mentioned in his address at the presentation of the Charlemagne Prize. In 1955 Przywara had warned of the temptation, driven by the technical-instrumental thinking that dominates us, to surrender to the logic of ideologies, whether capitalist or socialist, that tend to identify the Kingdom of God with particular forms of politics or government. These ideologies tend to sacralize their own systems and interests, thereby distorting the authentic meaning of the Kingdom of God and of messianism in the politics of the historical Jesus. Such a surrender would lead to relapsing into the expansionist and totalitarian game of many regimes.

Hence the pope proposes a political analysis of geography based on a non-political mediation. His will be the sociocultural mediation of peoples. This explains why Francis grants primacy to sociocultural processes as opposed to the occupation of political and pastoral spaces. The Church is called to energize sociocultural processes through its presence among many peoples and their cultures, holding as its central paradigm Christ, whom we should present not as an ethical model but as one who configures and gives form to our humanity. And the Church must do so "in its totality as people—*totus populus*—truly earthly, human, weak, and sinful, always and ever the new 'disfigured body' of the 'disfigured Christ' (as St. Augustine puts it). In this mystery, ultimately, every Christian is 'fully child and heir of God'—*totus filius*—and thus simply 'poor sinner'—*totus peccator.*"[22]

From Rafael Tello Francis learned that if the Church wishes to be faithful to the God revealed by Jesus it cannot build an ecclesial culture. From Erich Przywara he likewise learned that it cannot fall into the new aim of creating an alternative Christian culture that ends up resembling closed totalitarianisms and systems that exclude whoever does not belong to them. The credibility of the Church will not come from its strength, or its power as domination, but from "assuming itself a sinner" and "going out from its own center" to move toward the other, to the one different from itself, to the one who is at the edges. In Przywara's words: "The 'Israel of God' of the New Covenant was chosen solely as God's 'instrument' in order to 'go out,' again and again, 'from its own land and from the house of its fathers.' This is what the letter to the Hebrews says for Christians: 'to go out of the sheepfold of the Covenant and thus bear the opprobrium of Christ.'"[23] Thus, only a *church going out* is able to overcome the centuries-long temptation to make itself the center and to base its life on simply occupying spaces and positions.

This intuition coincides with Pius XII's vision of *de-Europeanizing* the Church and not perpetuating its imperial logic.[24] Erich Przywara had seen the need to give way to new, not closed-in or totalitarian, processes in history that could overcome the failed model of Christendom built by Charlemagne. Pius XII opened the possibility of moving the Church in that direction by shifting the center toward the peripheries. He spoke of this in his famous Christmas Message of 1946, where he expressed his view of the new world situation and articulated his desire to universalize the Church. With this in mind he expanded the College of Cardinals to include members from the United States, Canada, Africa, Asia, and Latin America in order to represent the largest possible number of peoples.

Certainly this was a historic intuition. Although it did not succeed in changing the ecclesial mindset, its great value lay in its having opened the debate on what the catholic and incarnate essence of the Church means. Pius XII went so far as to say that in this new era the Church must be seen to be an institution in the midst of the peoples, taking on their cultural reality, the truly human that is revealed in them, and consequently letting itself be evangelized by those who were once on the peripheries. It is these new places, far from Europe, that are to become the center, with their own genius. The Church must look to them and take its bearings from them. The idea was set forth in 1946:

> The Church lives and develops in all countries in the world, and all countries in the world contribute to its life and development. In other times, the life of the Church, in its visible aspect, deployed its strength principally in the countries of old Europe from which it extended like a majestic river to what could be called the periphery of the world. Today, on the contrary, it presents itself as an exchange of life and energy between all members of the mystical body of Christ on

earth. Many countries on other continents...have gone beyond the missionary stage of ecclesiastical organization; they are governed by their own hierarchy and they give the entire Church spiritual and material goods, whereas previously they only received them. This progress and this enrichment of the supernatural and even the social life of humanity, do they not reveal the true meaning of the supranationality of the Church? This supranationality is not maintained as though suspended at an inaccessible and intangible distance above the nations; on the contrary, as Christ was in the midst of men, the Church in which Christ is still living is found in the midst of the peoples. As Christ assumed a true human nature, the Church assumes the fullness of everything that is authentically human, and by raising it up, makes of it a spring of supernatural strength, regardless of the form in which it is found.[25]

Pius XII had a clear understanding of the new world situation. Europe was no longer the center of the world. The European millennium initiated by Charlemagne had come to an end, and the traditional center was beginning to be displaced toward a new ecumene. A worldwide ecclesial multipolarity was needed in order to respond to the new times. Because of its supranational character, the Church could not be identified with any particular culture, because it had to stand in the midst of all cultures, including, never excluding. "Its supranationality does not act like an empire extending its tentacles in all directions eying world domination."[26]

The path that it traces in its progress and expansion is contrary to the one followed by modern imperialism.

The Church makes progress primarily in depth; then in extension and breadth. It seeks first the human being; it devotes itself to forming human beings, to shaping and perfecting in them the divine likeness. Its work is done in the heart of each one, but it has its repercussion throughout the entire duration of life, in all areas of each one's activity. With human beings thus formed, the Church prepares for human society a foundation on which it can rest securely. Modern imperialism, on the other hand, follows an opposite path. It proceeds in extension and breadth. It does not seek the human being as such, but rather the things and the forces it makes the human being serve; it thereby bears in itself seeds that place in jeopardy the basis of shared human life.[27]

Francis understands the importance of this intuition of Pius XII. It is similar to the claim of Przywara, who understood that the Europe of the first centuries was born under the form of a *sacrum imperium* [holy empire] whose roots can be found in Charlemagne's attempt to create a Christian cultural totalitarianism. Thus, it is not enough to simply increase the number of cardinals from other nations and cultures; it is rather their ways of living and thinking, their sociocultural mediations, that must be incorporated into the Church's actions and deeds, as Methol Ferré insisted throughout the course of his ecclesial activity in Latin America.

A geopolitics at the service of peoples and their cultures

A new model demands that the peripheries be placed at the center, in a multiform and intercultural relationship. It entails rethinking the relationship of the Church-peoples-state triad. When we say "peoples" we have in mind their cultures, their ways of life, considered in relation to the Christian message. Here Francis follows the vision of Methol Ferré, who lived through the post-council deliberations and vicissitudes of the Latin American Church. In a volume edited by CELAM for a seminar on the theology of culture held in 1973, Ferré explained that

> the mission of the Church implies at the same time peoples and states. This triad, people, Church and state, is inseparable, and to consider them apart from each other, without their radical mutual insertion, is a too-common error that leads us into the blind alleys of an irresponsible idealism. Christ sends his followers to convert the nations, but the Church cannot by itself take over states. Quite a puzzle! It is a people, but it is not to be confused with peoples, since it exists only in them. It is supreme authority, but it isn't the state, and it lives only in states, subject to their rules, observing them, but not making them its own...It seems impossible to pile on more paradoxes. In natural terms [the Church] has the most precarious, weakest historical existence, but nevertheless the entire meaning of history converges toward it.[28]

How then are we to speak about this triad in terms of a sociocultural model?

In his first address to the ambassadors to the Vatican, Francis began by defining his role in these terms: "One of the titles of the Bishop of Rome is Pontiff, that is, a builder of bridges with God and between people. My wish is that the dialogue between us should help to build bridges connecting all people, in such a way that everyone can see in the other not an enemy, not a rival, but a brother or sister to be welcomed and embraced!"[29] Thus, the way of dialogue is posed as the route for reaching "agreements in which we all agree on something."[30] Otherwise, all that will be left will be resignation before those who impose, those who do not know how to build bridges, but only barriers. The ultimate goal is that the human subject live, and live well, that human beings enjoy a good life, that is, that they be accepted as brothers and sisters and integrated into society as equals, as individuals, rather than be subjected to the frightful play of polarization and discrimination that always converts the other, the one who is different, into object and instrument. This goal can be achieved if we work together to establish "political life on a truly human basis" (*GS* 73) and to build a society in which none feel that they are victims of the "throwaway culture,"[31] as the pope said in his apostolic journey to México.

Under the influence of Methol Ferré, Lucio Gera, and other theologians, many discussions and seminars held by CELAM were devoted to devising a theology of culture. The Church cannot replace economics or politics, nor can it provide them with formulas. What the Church, from its supranational and evangelical position, can offer peoples and states is a vision, one that can set in motion processes and narratives of recognition of the absolute value of human dignity. The Church can clearly affirm the need inherent in every person to be a subject, and make it clear that everything else must be aimed at attaining this end: *how to be subjects today.*[32]

It is in this undertaking that the pope, in his role as bridge builder, is called to contribute all that he can in order to rebuild the social bonds lost in hypermodernity, as he does in addresses during his apostolic journeys. As pontiff, his role is that of healing and redeeming the effects of exclusion.

Hence his journeys point to the open wound of the great problems of humankind, those that affect the majority and are caused by a minority.

But ecclesial geopolitics would be inconsequential without gospel discernment rooted in the praxis of Jesus, that is, as the practice of a soteriology of mercy in an intercultural and interreligious key. That is what the bishops, faithful to the council spirit, proposed in Aparecida. The then cardinal Bergoglio, head of the team that drafted the concluding document, made this the overriding theological theme: the fact that salvation takes place in history.[33] This is something that he has been demonstrating in action through the choice of the countries and places that he visits and from which he speaks to the globalized world. As he explained in his address to the ambassadors to the Holy See:

> Mercy was the common thread linking my apostolic journeys in the course of the past year. This was the case above all with my visit to Sarajevo, a city deeply scarred by the war in the Balkans and the capital of a country, Bosnia and Herzegovina, which is uniquely significant for Europe and for the entire world. As a crossroads of cultures, nations and religions, it is working successfully to build new bridges, to encourage those things that unite, and to see differences as opportunities for growth in respect for all. This is possible thanks to a patient and trusting dialogue capable of embracing the values of each culture and accepting the good that comes from the experience of others. I think too of my Journey to Bolivia, Ecuador and Paraguay, where I encountered peoples who have not given up in the face of difficulties, and who are

facing with courage, determination and solidarity
their many challenges, beginning with widespread
poverty and social inequality. During my Journey to
Cuba and the United States of America, I was able to
embrace two countries that were long divided and
that have decided to write a new page of history, em-
barking on the path of closer ties and reconciliation.[34]

Such newness can occur only if sociocultural processes and
mediations are safeguarded as places of historical action and
revelation. Francis proposes that we look through the lens of
his pastoral geopolitics at the service of peoples and their cultures; he asks us to do hermeneutics out of the "pluriform harmony" (*EG* 220) that springs from the culture of encounter;
hence his commitment to intercultural and interreligious sociopolitical dialogue. Just as evangelization will be connected
with the effort to preserve and foster cultural diversity as opposed to any form of indoctrination, likewise geopolitical po-
sitioning will be critical of any foreign intervention.

One of the clearest statements Bergoglio has made regarding geopolitics can be found in the prologue he wrote in
2005 for a book by the Uruguayan essayist Guzmán Carriquiry, titled *Una apuesta por América Latina* [A Wager for
Latin America]. In that prologue he explains that:

the solidity of the culture of the American peoples is
fundamentally threatened and weakened by two currents of weak thinking. One, which we could call the
imperial conception of globalization, conceives of it
as a perfect, polished sphere. All peoples are merged
in a uniformity that eliminates the tension between
particularities. [Robert Hugh] Benson foresaw this in

his famous novel *Lord of the World*. Such a view of globalization constitutes the most dangerous totalitarianism of postmodernity. True globalization must not be seen as a sphere, but as a polyhedron: the facets (uniqueness of peoples) preserve their identity and particularity, but they are united in tension, harmoniously seeking the common good. The other threatening current is that which, in everyday jargon, we could call "adolescent progressivism": a kind of enthusiasm for progress that is drained in mediations, frustrating the possibility of sensible and solid progress related to the roots of the people. This adolescent progressivism shapes the cultural colonialism of empires and is connected to the notion of the secularity of the state, which is actually militant secularism. These two postures constitute anti-popular, anti-national, anti-Latin American snares, although they are sometimes disguised with "progressive" masks.[35]

If the dominant tendency of the globalization process constitutes the most dangerous totalitarianism of our age, what are we to do? May we perhaps speak of a third way? How does the current pope understand his role in this new world dis-order? The first thing is to understand the primacy of the cultures of peoples vis-à-vis politics and economics. These latter always flow from cultures, but they are not their sources.[36] That is, they cannot be absolutized or ideologized, because they would kill the very source of their life and meaning, leaving peoples in a state of being subjected to oppression and domination with no transcendence. For this reason Francis proposes a sociopolitical narrative and gestures that safeguard the *ethos* of peoples, their ethico-mythico soul or heart, as something sacred.[37]

This does not mean absolutizing or idealizing the people, or moralizing their choices and decisions, but it does mean regarding the people as being a center and hermeneutical locus, as opposed to being peripheral and instrumental. It means valuing social justice by privileging labor over capital and refusing to absolutize state, party, or money. Although taking the side of freedom can be understood in terms of individualism, as is done by neoliberal capitalism, that is, autarkic and with no moral discernment, it should be aimed at strengthening and fostering the bonds or ties that show us how to be human beings, those ties that constitute us as a diverse, non-biological family comprised of many peoples and cultures. That can be achieved only if we overcome the "educated elite" mindset that views the people as lacking in culture and training, only if we take them on as subjects with their own way of being and acting. Only then can we achieve the true common good.[38]

Unleashing processes and dynamics

The pope regards geopolitics as a kind of pastoral praxis[39] that anticipates[40] what life would be if it were lived with justice and mercy, on the principle of never giving up anything as lost.[41] Such is the grace of one who believes in and lives mercy as the power to change and who calls for the redemption of the existing state of injustice. As Francis said in Mexico: "Let us together ask our God for the gift of conversion, the gift of tears. Let us ask him to give us open hearts like those of the Ninevites, who were open to his call heard in the suffering faces of countless men and women. No more death! No more exploitation! There is always time to change, always a way out, and always an opportunity; there is always time to implore the mercy of God."[42] This is a way of guiding history toward the Kingdom, even now; it is the sociopolitical moment lived in eschatological anticipation of the ultimate truths of our collective existence. In the words of Antonio Spadaro, SJ, it is about "never considering anything or anyone as definitively lost in relations between nations, peoples, and states."[43] It is when geopolitics is placed at the service of the Gospel—not of a religious ideology—that it becomes pastoral ministry and is lived ecclesially as a part of the processes of evangelizing culture.

The emphasis, accordingly, must not be on negotiating spaces and positions of temporal power, but on generating, in our own historical situation, processes of a sociocultural nature that can reorient time toward its fullness, toward the Kingdom, through gestures and sociopolitical actions that seek to make us neighbors to others. Francis explained this in his visit to Paraguay, where he said that in order to build this alternate model the Christian community must be "inserted and incarnate in the national experience of the people and discern the liberating or saving action of the Church from the perspective of the people and their interests."[44] People are not mere receptacles and objects of outside projects thought up by others outside them:

> The world's peoples want to be artisans of their own destiny. They want to advance peacefully toward justice. They do not want forms of tutelage or interference by which those with greater power subordinate those with less. They want their culture, their language, their social processes, and their religious traditions to be respected. No actual or established power has the right to deprive peoples of the full exercise of their sovereignty. Whenever they do so, we

see the rise of new forms of colonialism that seriously lessen the possibility for peace and justice.[45]

Francis goes on to explain the term "pluriform harmony," praising the "efforts to bring peoples and cultures together in a form of coexistence" that he calls "polyhedric," *where each group preserves its own identity by building together a plurality that does not threaten but rather reinforces unity.*[46] This occurs when we see the people as agent, that is, when we live as citizens within a people and together we build a culture of encounter in pluriform harmony.

What humanizes is not simply recognition of a pluricultural reality, which would be limited to respect for spaces acquired and gained socioculturally and politically in terms of rights, in particular political rights. What actually humanizes is *intercultural and interreligious interaction and integration* between the different groups coexisting in a society, the symbiosis that is generated in a horizontal relationship, built on a first-name basis of subject to subject. Interculturality is the measure of the attainment of a true culture of encounter lived as "pluriform harmony" (*EG* 220), when we then understand that "time is greater than space," and thus our vision should not be limited by the space we happen to occupy.

The struggle for rights does not end when the condition of citizenship is reached. That struggle continues, because it requires setting in motion sociocultural and historical processes that encourage a culture of encounter in place of sectarianism, segregation, or exclusion. "True cultures are never closed in on themselves—cultures would die if they closed in on themselves—but are called to meet other cultures and to create new realities. When we study history we find ancient cultures that no longer exist. They have died, and for many reasons. But one of them is having closed themselves in."[47]

What is proposed is a process of *intercultural symbiosis*, and therefore of *growth in humanity*, on the basis of a global human kinship. The image with which Francis represents this alternative model "is not then the sphere which stifles, nor isolated partiality, which proves barren,"[48] but, as we have previously noted, the polyhedron. On this point Francis constructs an entire geopolitical and pastoral praxis at the service of peoples and their cultures. Its two leading themes are intercultural sociopolitical dialogue and interreligious dialogue, all within the framework of a unity that does not make everything uniform.[49] As he stated in his apostolic journey to Paraguay:

> Dialogue must be built on something, an identity. For example, I think about the dialogue we have in the Church, interreligious dialogue, where different representatives of religions speak to each other. We sometimes meet to speak and share our points of view, and everyone speaks on the basis of their own identity: "I'm Buddhist, I'm Evangelical, I'm Orthodox, I'm Catholic." Each one explains their identity. They do not negotiate their identity. This means that, for there to be dialogue, that fundamental basis of identity must exist. And what is the identity of a country? (and here we are speaking about a social identity): to love the nation. The nation first, and then my business! The nation comes first! That is identity. That is the basis upon which I will dialogue. If I am to speak without that basis, without that identity, then dialogue is pointless. Moreover, dialogue presupposes and demands that we seek a culture of

encounter; an encounter that acknowledges that diversity is not only good, it is necessary.[50]

Let us recall again that Francis is influenced by Lucio Gera with his theology of historical processes and personal lives. Based on this theological approach, the current geopolitical vision of the Church is not a mere strategic vision for the sake of its own power, or for world domination, as it was in times past. The ecclesiastical institution is called to follow the Spirit of Jesus who accompanies and promotes the processes of humanization among brothers and sisters, and of salvation in history, because "all growth in humanity brings us closer to reproducing the image of the Son so that He will be the firstborn among many brothers."[51] This is in fact the primary purpose of the pastoral geopolitics of Francis. Doing everything we can so that there will be no more "excluded" is a theological option; it is in line with God's will to create and with the praxis of Jesus.[52] In short, "the reality and the response to this reality is at the heart of the Gospel, specifically because, as we see in Matthew 25, the attitude we adopt when faced with this reality is what we will be judged on in the end."[53]

Forming citizens within a people

In the 1970s Argentina lived through conflicts in society and serious divisions within the Catholic Church. As is well known, a significant number of clergy and religious supported Peronism. In his opening address to the Sixteenth Provincial Congregation of the Jesuits in 1974, the future pope spoke of his "conviction that it is necessary to go beyond sterile internal church contradictions so that we can enlist in a genuine apostolic strategy that can identify the real enemy and marshal our forces against it." Bergoglio devoted himself to rethinking directions for the nation and for the Church. With that in mind, he wanted to foster a unity greater than that which Argentina was experiencing at the time, with the understanding that the common good, which is "the whole," is more important than each individual stance and option, to which he refers as "the parts." The topic of building this greater unity or common good began to appear as central in the theology that was inspiring him and was to guide him in the geopolitical decisions he would make and the narrative that he would later advocate as Pope.

What criteria need to be taken into account in order to achieve this greater unity and common good with which politics ought to be imbued?

We can gain insight into this by tracing the development of the future pope's thought. First, and very realistically, he understood that unity is not attained as long as there is a temptation to sidestep conflicts rather than taking them on. He calls this kind of attitude "spiritualizing abstractionism." Second, it is likewise not achieved if economic and public policies antithetical to Christian ends are applied, as for example when Marxist or classical liberal ideological visions are imposed by groups that hold political, economic, or religious power. He calls this the temptation of a "functionalist focus on methodology" and "abstract ideologies." Third, it is necessary to avoid "ethicizing" or "moralizing" postures, that is, those that "isolate conscience from lived reality and that draw up plans that are formal and abstract as opposed to concrete and practical." He calls these postures "priestly platitudes." That is how he explained matters in his speech at the Seventh Workshop on Pastoral Social Ministry in Buenos Aires, in 2005.[54]

Five years later, in the conference he gave on Argentina's bicentenary of independence in 2010, he went on to add a fourth criterion necessary for achieving unity and the common good, "reality is more than idea," which implies the primacy of the person over ideologies or systems of thought. But it is only out of *closeness*, out of making oneself neighbor to the other, that reality overcomes idea. As Francis explained in Cuba, "this caring for others out of love is not about being servile. Rather, it means putting the question of our brothers and sisters at the center. Service always looks to their faces, touches their flesh, senses their *closeness* and even, in some cases, 'suffers' that closeness and tries to help them. Service is never ideological, for we do not serve ideas, we serve people."[55]

All these criteria that Bergoglio was formulating "help to resolve the challenge of being a citizen and belonging to a society."[56] As pope he continually returns to them in the encyclical *Lumen Fidei* (*LF* 55, 57) and in the apostolic exhortation *Evangelii Gaudium* (*EG* 217–237), as well as in his many addresses and homilies. Taken together these criteria seek to create the dynamic by which the inhabitants of a nation may move toward living, one and all, as citizens within a people, constituted as community agents, for only thus will it be possible to overcome both fragmenting and isolating individualism and stifling and leveling collectivism:

> People in every nation enhance the social dimension of their lives by acting as committed and responsible citizens, not as a mob swayed by the powers that be. Let us not forget that "responsible citizenship is a virtue, and participation in political life is a moral obligation." Yet becoming a people demands something

more. It is an ongoing process in which every new generation must take part: a slow and arduous effort calling for a desire for integration and a willingness to achieve this through the growth of a peaceful and multifaceted culture of encounter.[57]

Becoming a people entails achieving true interculturality in which one's personal identity is integrated with that of others to form a new collective human reality that does not suppress but rather enriches each part in a "we." From this reciprocity a new identity springs forth in the form of a *multifaceted harmony*. The call of the then cardinal Bergoglio was to "refound social bonds, appeal to the ethics of solidarity, and generate a culture of encounter," capable of applying the brakes to the growing culture of fragmentation promoted by globalization.[58] In his address on Argentina's bicentenary he invoked the words from the document *Church and National Community* written by the Argentine bishops in 1981, recalling how "each sector has exalted the values that it represents and the interests it defends, excluding other groups." In his talk he went on to discuss how restoring true human development entails self-recognition as people/nation, because "the people are the citizenry—committed, reflective, conscious, united behind a common objective or project." That is something to which the Church is called to contribute, whether pastorally or geopolitically, as in fact all religions are, as Francis stated in his apostolic journey to Kenya.[59]

Citizenship is thus not an individual condition of the human person. It is a social and communal condition of persons that makes them the subject of duties and rights, as stated in the *Puebla Document* (503, 1291), and that enables persons to be fully integrated into national and international life.[60] But its fullest meaning is achieved on the basis of brother/sisterliness as the essence of belonging to a people, imbibing its values and traditions, projecting itself toward a common destiny with others. Herein lies the value of the commitment made by the Latin American bishops in Puebla to understand and face the challenge of the journey toward interculturality, in which the new subjects of today and their cultures strive toward integration (*Puebla* 408). The goal is to seek the integration—not the assimilation—of all those who are not yet regarded as true citizens, making sure that they do not lose their own sociocultural *ethos*, that which confers meaning and transcendence, rootedness and interiority. In short, faced with cultural globalization, geopolitics is critical for restoring social bonds and cultural identities, because it involves seeking confluence between peoples and their cultures. "It is the convergence of peoples who, within the universal order, maintain their own individuality; it is the sum total of persons within a society which pursues the common good, which truly has a place for everyone" (*EG* 236).

5

From Ecclesial Culture to Personal Encounter with Jesus

Francis and the spirit of Vatican II

What is new about Francis is that he has been putting into practice the spirit of Vatican II. That spirit was being lost in a gradual process of restorationist regression, starting with the papacy of John Paul II. This led to what was called an ecclesial winter, which culminated in the exemplary and virtuous resignation of Benedict XVI. The major motifs of the council also define the ministry of Francis. Thus, a new period of ecclesial springtime has begun, and it has awakened hope among many who were discouraged and forgotten, like sheep without a shepherd.[1] Its impact has not been expressed primarily in drawing people to the ecclesiastical institution. With his humanizing message, so like that of Jesus, Francis reaches out to all hearts, without regard to their moral, economic, sociocultural, or religious differences. The actions of Francis have helped to desacralize an institution that, since the time of Constantine, had presented itself as sacred and untouchable. Following the spirit of the council, Francis has responded to the signs of the time with creative fidelity, trying to do what Jesus would do today in our contemporary history.[2] Francis says this himself:

> Vatican II was a re-reading of the Gospel in light of contemporary culture. Vatican II produced a renewal movement that comes simply from the same Gospel. Its fruits are enormous. Just recall the liturgy. The work of liturgical reform has been a service to the people as a re-reading of the Gospel from a concrete historical situation. Yes, there are hermeneutics of continuity and discontinuity, but one thing is clear: the dynamic of reading the Gospel, actualizing its message for today—which was typical of Vatican II— is absolutely irreversible.[3]

In pointing his ministry in that direction, Francis has been able to overcome both the temptation to a utopian projection of a Church that lives only from promise and the future and the temptation to a restorationist vision of an institution that only yearns for the past. In both of these cases we would be dealing with a Church that does not live in the present, that locates itself outside the current global age, and that doesn't know how to respond to the signs of our present reality.

As Francis thinks about the present condition of human beings today, it is in the light of the gospels and with an understanding of the mission of the Church as the people of God in the midst of the peoples of the earth,[4] not above them. As he says, "Every utopian (future-oriented) or restorationist (past-oriented) impulse is spiritually unhealthy. God is real and he shows himself in the 'today'...The 'today' is closest to eternity; even more: the 'today' is a flash of eternity. In the 'today' eternal life is played out."[5]

Many may wonder why Francis's recovery of the council spirit is so important. We cannot forget that Vatican II marked an extraordinary shift in the self-understanding of the church community and in the way the fundamental truths of the faith were expressed. It was an event that moved the Church beyond the borders of the traditional ways in which it had seen itself, setting in motion a process of *aggiornamento* for the entire direction of the Church, both pastorally and structurally.[6] The council came to recognize that "the future of humanity lies in the hands of those who are strong enough to provide coming generations with reasons for living and hoping."[7] We can imagine what a statement like this would have meant in the years before the council, where any attempt at reform and dialogue with the modern world was rejected out of hand.

After a centuries-long history of ecumenical councils that had formulated dogmas and condemned heresies, Pope John XXIII in his inaugural address on October 11, 1962, dared to broach the topic of a new direction needed to respond to the new spirit of the age: "Christ our Lord said: '*Seek first the Kingdom of God and His justice*,' and this word 'first' indicates what the primary direction of all our thoughts and energies must be." Reflection on the relationship between the Church and the world in light of fidelity to the Kingdom of God leads to the realization that the ecclesial community must exist in the world, "living and acting with it."[8] The new orientation that the Church ought to assume was clear: to share with all human beings the good news of God revealed in Jesus Christ starting from the conditions in which we live, for "the joys and the hopes, the grief and the anguish of the people of this age, especially those who are poor or in any way afflicted, these are the joys and hopes, the grief and anguish of the followers of Christ. Indeed, nothing genuinely human fails to raise an echo in their hearts."[9]

Thus it is clear that we must return to the spirit of Jesus, which entails being "at the service of humankind"[10] as people of God journeying toward building "universal kinship," for "the human person deserves to be preserved; human society deserves to be renewed. Hence the focal point [must] be the human person, whole and entire, body and soul, heart and conscience, mind and will."[11] It is imperative that we consider concrete human subjects and locate ourselves in their life-world.

The ecclesial community must see itself in terms of discipleship, which finds its paradigm in the God of Jesus and its strength and inspiration in his Spirit. It is "a community of people united in Christ and guided by the Holy Spirit in their journey to the Kingdom of their Father and they have welcomed the news of salvation meant for all of humanity."[12] That is why the council addresses "the whole of humanity"[13] and not just Christians, because in this fashion the Church "believes it can contribute greatly toward making the human family and its history still more human"[14] as an expression of its fidelity to the Kingdom of God. Such a vision calls the Church to recover its condition of discipleship. Thus, inspired by the insights of Aparecida, Francis states that we are all missionary disciples, not as a simple function of being Christians, but as what defines our very being, ever going out to the other: "Every Christian is a missionary to the extent that he or she has encountered the love of God in Christ Jesus: we no longer say that we are 'disciples' and 'missionaries,' but rather that we are always 'missionary disciples,'[15] that is, always going out and searching, never closed in on ourselves, 'in our little chapels.'"[16]

A change of ecclesial model

The Jesuit cardinal Robert Bellarmine (1542–1621), one of the great defenders of the Church in response to the Protestant Reformation in the sixteenth century, said in his work, *Disputationes de controversiis christianae fidei adversus hujus temporis haereticos*,[17] that "this one and true Church is the assembly of men bound together by the profession of the same Christian faith and the communion of the same sacraments, under the rule of the legitimate pastors, and especially that of the Roman Pontiff, the one Vicar of Christ on earth." This post-Tridentine notion presented a model of Christian community that thought of itself almost exclusively in terms of its being in itself and for itself—what Francis criticizes as a self-referential and self-centered church—on the basis of the visible elements that expressed its genetic and structural unity (profession of faith, sacraments, legitimate pastors). By reason of this it sustained its own credibility and proposed itself as the means by which believers could live out their faith. Grace was something undeserved and unmerited that could be received only by believing what the Church declared and operating as it operated. Under this arrangement, believers are only objects, addressees who participate in ritual and go to church, but they are not the agents of their own process of humanization nor do they have anything of their own to contribute as active subjects.

For many Christians this is still the model for encounter with God: through the mediation of an ecclesial culture as opposed to the living out of a gospel life based on a relationship with the person of Jesus[18] and not on structures or disciplinary reforms. There needs to be a return to a Christianity in which personal encounter with the Jesus of the gospels is the axis around which Christian life revolves.

Such an understanding would replace the prevailing clerical mindset with one that is more horizontal and familial. Francis understands that to arrive at this the Church must undergo a paradigm shift by which it ceases being self-referential[19] or self-centered.[20] By no longer reflecting its own light but rather the light of Christ, the Church de-centers itself;[21] it leaves the safe places; it goes out to the peripheries, to those whom the world discards, those whom the world today regards as surplus.[22] That is how ecclesial culture can experience conversion.

The Jesuit Karl Rahner warned of the danger of ecclesial culture when he said, "The modern Catholic lives, one might say, according to the awareness of the Church expressed in the First Vatican Council. The characteristic quality of this awareness lies in the fact that the its particular emphasis (and not, of course, its exclusive emphasis) is on the Church regarded as a motive, empirically and experientially, of credibility and not on the Church as an object (in itself) of faith."[23] The fact is that the Christian "has the experience of having the Church as an object of faith, but not of believing *in* the Church, i.e., he experiences it as the object but not as the ultimate ground of faith."[24] The Church is only a means, a mediation whereby we believe as a community of believers, but what gives it its raison d'être and enables it to carry out its historical and perceptible function is the personal faith of each believer *in* Jesus of Nazareth."[25] Rahner concludes: "The message of what is to come (and this is the Church) cannot be the actual reality of what is to come; the Church in time is not as great as the eternal Kingdom of God."[26]

Accordingly, the Church cannot be considered sacred, as something sacralized, capable of speaking on behalf of God and thus replacing the foundational relationship of each believer with Jesus, the event that gives form to his or her life and endows it with meaning. As we are reminded by some texts of the Latin American magisterium: "Only Jesus is absolute and model of Christian living, which relativizes any historical expression of relationship with Him, just as adhesion to Him makes one a new human being."[27] Any historical form of encounter with God, such as the Church, is relativized[28] and it is called to find itself with Jesus as the sole Lord of history, above all other (political, economic, religious) lords and powers, or other mediations or practices of piety that seek to replace the saving personal relationship with the God who is revealed to us through the humanity of Jesus.[29]

Francis says as much in *Evangelii Gaudium* with the following words: "I never tire of repeating those words of Benedict XVI which take us to the very heart of the Gospel: 'Being a Christian is not the result of an ethical choice or a lofty idea, but the encounter with an event, a person, which gives life a new horizon and a decisive direction.'"[30] For the pope, the route to being Christian is that of the gospels, which no doctrine or church practice can replace: "We must ensure that the habitual activities of all Christian communities, in the parishes, associations, and movements, truly have at heart the personal encounter with Christ communicated to us in His Word since, as St. Jerome teaches, 'ignorance of the Scriptures is ignorance of Christ' (*Dei Verbum* 25)." In other words, says Francis, "The question we have to ask ourselves . . . is if and how we too are open to being challenged by the Gospel; whether the Gospel is truly the 'manual' for our daily living and the decisions we are called to make."[31]

But this is not a generic or abstract matter, devoid of historical reality. We are called to "seek first the Kingdom of God"[32] in this world, from within—within history, and from below—for the sake of the poor and excluded. The Jesus-

event is not detectable in those who believe that salvation occurs despite history or that we live outside it. This is what
Francis means when he says that the encounter with Jesus
takes place at the peripheries of our world. Indeed, the council spirit recognizes that grace works through the action of
the Spirit and not by explicit confession in Jesus. As Rahner
said, one can be a Christian "even though one does not know
the name of Christ or thinks one has to reject it,"[33] because
"through this Spirit, who is 'the pledge of our inheritance'
(Eph 1:14), the whole man is renewed from within [i.e.,
within the human condition of historical embodiedness and
sociocultural environment], until the redemption of the body
(Rom 8:23)[34] is achieved."

This dynamic of the Kingdom de-centers the Church. It
reminds us that a church community is not credible by itself,
but only insofar as it follows the brother/sisterly humanity of
Jesus of Nazareth, giving itself to non-believers, the poor, the
unfortunate, the despised, the abused, those who have other
beliefs and different values. But the brother/sisterly construction of society, as expression of universal salvation, is not
simply about becoming involved in a social endeavor or a
philanthropic endeavor. It is not a problem that can be solved
by technology or by socioeconomic development. Rather
"brotherly dialogue among men does not reach its perfection
on the level of technical progress, but on the deeper level of
interpersonal relationships. These demand a mutual respect
for the full spiritual dignity of the person."[35]

This is about living in accordance with what God the
Creator has willed with regard to the goods of the earth:
these goods are intended for sharing, for enabling us to grow
as a human family so as to find eternal life and build the
Kingdom of God in this world. We recall the wonderful
words of *Gaudium et Spes*: "This communitarian character is

developed and consummated in the work of Jesus Christ, for the very Word made flesh willed to share in human fellowship. He was present at the wedding of Cana, visited the house of Zacchaeus, ate with publicans and sinners. He revealed the love of the Father and humanity's sublime calling in terms of the most common of social realities and by making use of the speech and the imagery of plain everyday life. Willingly obeying the laws of his country he sanctified human ties, especially family ones, which are the source of social structures. He chose to lead the life proper to an artisan of his time and place."[36] Hence, "In his preaching he clearly taught the sons of God to treat one another as brothers,"[37] so that "the human race would become the Family of God, in which the fullness of the Law would be love."[38]

As institution, as we have explained, the Church is not the subject of faith (*credere in ecclesiam*), but rather the object of faith (*credere ecclesiam*). Only the God who is revealed to us through the humanity of Jesus of Nazareth is the subject of faith (*credere in Deum*), because faith entails a personal and personalizing relationship (*in carne*) in which we are constituted definitively, fully, and eternally as children of the same Father who is in heaven. Otherwise, the Church would cease being *sacramentum*, because it is a sign that signifies not itself but the mystery of God, as revealed in Jesus of Nazareth (*res significata*).[39]

The Church, therefore, shares the good news of salvation through the life of its members.[40] We cannot think of it as something absolute or generic, which has itself as its own foundation and purpose, for it is not eternal or complete; rather it is called to holiness (Rom 1:7; Eph 5:27), which will be expressed through the capacity that it develops to generate kinship relationships within a gathered community. It is in these kinship relationships that the gathered community

(Church) must find its support in the midst of the most dramatic adversities, for it lives as a community of pilgrims in whose mutual love it finds the hope to keep journeying as follower of the Messiah. It must be a "community of faith, hope and love" (*LG* 8). That is why its members, the witnesses, become "the palpable [and] historical sign of credibility in the Church."[41] In other words, our love and brother-sisterly commitment is not *to* the Church, but *in* the Church (*fraternitas*) and *as* Church (*convocata*), that is, in the mutual relations of the true kinship of the daughters and sons of God.

Karl Rahner notes:

> But in contrast to previous ages, the Church remains the Church *for 'me' in particular* only when I believe. She really shows herself again more clearly, more painfully, more challengingly than ever before since the time of Constantine's Church as what she was and will be: the Church of believers, the church that exists because she is the object of faith, and is the object of faith because one believes in God through Jesus Christ.[42]

This means that today, more than ever, salvation history must be seen in terms of the implications and demands that lead to the salvation of each person in the light of the historical memory of the *verba, acta et passa in carne* of Jesus of Nazareth, the Son who reveals to us the love of the merciful Father. Salvation cannot be understood statically from the action of gathering or of belonging (*Mater Convocans*), but rather from ways of relating to one another and thus constituting brother and sister subjects within the congregation or assembly (*fraternitas convocata*). In this assembly, the Church is recognized as credible sign of salvation, because it witnesses to the Kingdom.[43] This is the route of the *via testimonii* which understands ecclesiology on the basis of Christology and soteriology based on faith rather than piety and devotion.

The future of the Christian believer is not the Church but the God of the Kingdom who is revealed in Jesus; and when he is all in all, the Church as institution and *Mater Convocans* will cease.[44] Only the *fraternitas convocata* will remain, the true kinship between the daughters and sons of God. Hence the urgent call made by Vatican II to "offer to humanity the honest assistance of the Church in fostering that brotherhood and sisterhood of all which corresponds to this destiny of theirs,"[45] that of every human person in his or her journey to salvation. There is no other way to know the divine presence than by way of the kinship among human beings along the path of becoming children of the living and true God, the God of the Kingdom, the God revealed through the humanity of Jesus. But conceiving of this kinship, understanding that our future is not the Church, but the Kingdom, requires that we discern the forms of ecclesial culture that reduce the faith to a mere disciplinary practice and that turn the believer into an ideological and indoctrinated being.

Ecclesial culture and the pathology of power

Rafael Tello understands ecclesial culture to mean "the more or less particular ways of action originating from a particular community, which give rise to a particular human nucleus, to styles and ways of thinking and interacting." Entering into ecclesial culture would mean "active belonging to particular communities such as parishes, membership in pious associations or works, the way the liturgical year is organized, public worship or reception of the sacraments, the manner of praying, a large portion of the prayers employed, works of penitence, etc."[46] This manner of living the faith, enclosed in small groups or bubbles of ecclesial culture, has led in recent years and especially among the younger generations to a crisis of meaning. The crisis has been felt in the transmission of the faith, in its modes, models, contents, and perspectives, insofar as these have been incapable of responding to the crisis generated by the current processes of globalization.

In 1981 Lucio Gera gave a conference sponsored by Caritas in Buenos Aires in which he presented this idea and argued that "the crisis of the world today is a crisis of global culture, a crisis of civilization."[47] He situated the crisis on three levels: "a crisis of meaning and value, which reflects a lack of wisdom"; "a crisis on the level of institutions and structures, in which not enough wisdom is translated"; and finally, "a crisis on the level of scientific-technical instruments which, without authentically human ends, turn anarchic and lead toward subhuman purposes."[48] In short, for Gera this is a crisis of "the global style in accordance with which human beings are living. It is not partial—merely economic, say, or political—but total, a crisis 'of the whole human being.'"[49] Hence the very transmission of the faith is conflicted, because it has lost its capacity to relate to contemporary culture.[50] Its unappealing modes and its content devoid of reference points lead to proposals empty of meaning that have only been able to adapt to, rather than transcending, the prevailing cultural models. The proposals lack any prophetic capacity and thus contribute to the continuing loss of ecclesial connection with the new realities. Along these lines, as Ratzinger writes, the upshot will be a deepening of the "gray pragmatism of the daily life of the church in which everything apparently continues normally, but in reality the faith is being consumed and falling into paltriness."[51]

This should move us to rethink the "evangelization of culture as evangelization of civilization, of the age, of the manners and styles of humankind," because what is under threat is not one dimension of human beings but their very dignity, meaning, and place in history and society. It is their condition as agents that is threatened. Faith teaches us to assume historical responsibility for the world, for society, for peoples and their cultures; it prepares the human person to be the agent of his or her own history and to share that responsibility with others. But it does so by helping people to understand that "getting out of the crisis does not depend merely on potentially favorable historical circumstances, but on the operations of the freedom of the human being,"[52] on personal decisions, as well as on the processes, actions, and orientations of meaning that may be produced.

Tello is clear in claiming that ecclesial culture[53] is foreign to the actual historical processes of peoples because it is concerned with winning and holding onto religious spaces, rather than with really connecting with the sufferings and hopes of ordinary human beings in their concrete secular history. This is because ecclesial culture is defined by ecclesial (not grassroots) communities, or by closed groups that gather only Christians on the basis of group affinities of a ritual and disciplinary—as opposed to a gospel—nature. In communities or groups of this kind, there is no room for discernment as a process promoting a personal and intimate encounter with God. The upshot is that this way of acting and passing on the faith becomes an end in itself for evangelization, whose only purpose is doctrinal transmission and the gathering of individuals as opposed to forming humanity.

At a the meeting with the CELAM Coordinating Committee on July 28, 2013, in Río de Janeiro, Francis spoke of some factors that need to be taken into account; he called them "temptations" because they arise from an ecclesial culture that grants primacy to the disciplinary and the juridical, to formal compliance, and to merely belonging to the institution, with no need for deeper familial bonds. He then described the temptations in light of the discernment that the Church itself, as a faithful people, should make if it wishes to foster a process of pastoral conversion and thus respond to our global situation. As he explained in Rio, these temptations include "making the gospel an ideology," "sociological reductionism," "psychologizing," "the Pelagian solution," "functionalism," and "clericalism." They are expressions of a deformed pathology of power that has contributed to and sustained among Christians the loss of their status as subjects and as free, co-responsible believers.

Such terms, coming from the lips of the pope and addressed to members of the very church power structure over which he presides, may sound very harsh. They make evident the urgency of the need for change, of a personal and structural conversion that involves questioning the spiritual manner in which we live the faith—that is, our fidelity to the Kingdom preached by Jesus as opposed to disciplinary power structures. It involves discerning where God and salvation are moving today. It involves our very image of God, because "ecclesial culture is marked by a particular spirituality in which God is seen in comparison with the world, from which springs the prevalence of a certain kind of religious attitudes."[54]

For people who have known and lived their faith only within the realm of ecclesial culture, God is not in the world but above it, an unattainable good, the supreme and constant judge of everything that human beings do. This is not the model of Christian life to be followed. It is faithful not to the praxis of Jesus but to the disciplinary command of a Church that has rendered itself incapable of connecting with the reality of the poor majority of humankind.

We can find a different model, as Tello explains, in the culture of the people, because "it is imbued with another spirituality in which God is seen in connection and continuity with the things of this life, from which even secular human activities and actions draw meaning and value."[55] It is what Lucio Gera explains when he discusses finding the presence of the Spirit today in the secular and temporal processes of history.[56] He speaks of discovering "the salvation-history projection of Christ and the Spirit in universal history, understood as secular history, which some call profane," adding that he has in mind "a theology of that history, or the knowledge of particular secular or temporal historical processes."[57] It is there, in this secular dimension of history, from which a new process of passing on the faith should be conceived and practiced. This soteriology allows for an understanding of the processes set in motion by the social movements of peoples, whose members are not always Christians, as subjects and agents of evangelization. Any ecclesial attempt to penetrate and transform society out of group bubbles or from the verticality of ecclesial culture will be in vain, because it will not be responding gratuitously, instinctively, to the life of faith, or—what amounts to the same thing—to the call of Matthew 25, which is nothing but the criterion of fidelity to the praxis of Jesus.

One of the most forceful criticisms made by Francis against the mindset behind such an ecclesial attempt, which springs from ecclesial culture and permeates all levels of the church institution, has to do with in what he calls the "complex of the elect," or the "pathology of ecclesial power." This is an attitude that arises in institutions for training clergy and religious, spreads out to parishes, and is strengthened through lifestyles not in tune with the prophetic dimension of church ministry. Francis criticizes those who view the calling to the priesthood or to religious life under a distorted theology of "vocation," according to which God separates a person from the world in order to set him or her on a level higher than that of other members of the Church. The result has been a paralyzed ecclesial structure that has been unable to discern or respond to the current signs of the times and seems, with its top-down view, to sidestep the dramatic situations affecting poor peoples, the great majority of humankind.

One result of the pathology of ecclesial culture is that its members run the risk of being reduced to "closed circles, where belonging to a clique becomes more important than belonging to the Body."[58] If this keeps happening, primacy will end up being given to "the parts" (ordained ministers, members of religious orders, intra-ecclesial groups and movements) rather than "to the whole" (people of God, faithful people, people/nation).

Vocation, the foundation of which is the baptism of all, is a service and a responsibility that must be exercised collegially, as Francis has emphasized by means of his own understanding the Petrine ministry.[59] Being chosen is not a privilege or a form of separation, much less license to exercise pastoral tyranny. If this is not well understood, it leads to so-called clericalism, which is a distortion of ecclesiastical power. This unfortunate pathology leads members of the institution to behave, in the pope's words, with "existential schizophrenia," which means loss of contact with reality, with actual people and their real problems. The consequence is that primacy is given to "occupying spaces" of power and to carrying out individual projects rather than to "unleashing processes" in response to people, especially the poorest and most needy. Indeed, clericalism creates the illusion of a parallel world in which there are no real needs or urgent problems but rather security and privileges, and where the other is treated as inferior and less worthy of salvation rather than as an autonomous agent already embraced by God's love. This is a style of life that favors ministerial mediocrity and feeds on self-serving, short-term relationships. In other words, it is a style that turns ministers into a "a caricature in which there is following without renunciation, prayer without encounter, fraternal life without communion, obedience without trust, and charity without transcendence."[60]

A first step toward achieving a "poor church for the poor" will be overcoming such "clericalism—this desire to lord it over lay people—which entails a mistaken and destructive separation of the clergy, a kind of narcissism."[61] In his 2014 message to the Roman Curia, Francis presented a brief phenomenological description of the unhealthy elements and distorted styles of Christian life that have been shaping the realm of ecclesial culture, and that must be overcome if we wish to retrieve the humanizing guidance of faithful presence in today's world under the inspiration of the Gospel. Here is a summary:

1. "The disease of thinking we are 'immortal,' 'immune' or downright 'indispensable,' neglecting the need for regular check-ups . . . The antidote to this plague is the grace of realizing that we are sinners and able to say heartily: 'We are unworthy servants. We have only done what was our duty' (Lk17:10)."

2. "Another disease is the 'Martha complex,' excessive busy-ness. It is found in those who immerse themselves in work and inevitably neglect 'the better part': sitting at the feet of Jesus (cf. Lk 10:38–42)."

3. "Then too there is the disease of mental and spiritual 'petrification'...! This is the disease of those who lose 'the sentiments of Jesus' (cf. Phil 2:5–11), because as time goes on their hearts grow hard and become incapable of loving unconditionally the Father and our neighbor (cf. Mt 22:34–35)."

4. "The disease of excessive planning and of functionalism...We contract this disease because it is always more easy and comfortable to settle in our own sedentary and unchanging ways. In truth, the Church shows her fidelity to the Holy Spirit to the extent that she does not try to control or tame him."

5. "The disease of poor coordination [when] members lose communion among themselves, the body loses its harmonious functioning."

6. "'Spiritual Alzheimer's disease'...a progressive decline in the spiritual faculties."

7. "The disease of rivalry and vainglory...when appearances, the color of our clothes and our titles of honor become the primary object in life, ... [we become] 'enemies of the cross of Christ' because 'they glory in their shame, with minds set on earthly things' (Phil 3:19)."

8. "The disease of existential schizophrenia...the disease of those who live a double life, the fruit of that hypocrisy typical of the mediocre and of a progressive spiritual emptiness..."

9. "The disease of gossiping, grumbling, and back-biting."

10. "The disease of idolizing superiors...of those who court their superiors in the hope of gaining their favor. They are victims of careerism and opportunism; they honor persons and not God (cf. Mt 23:8–12)."

11. "The disease of indifference to others."

12. "The disease of a lugubrious face...An apostle must make an effort to be courteous, serene, enthusiastic, and joyful, a person who transmits joy everywhere he goes."

13. "The disease of hoarding...When an apostle tries to fill an existential void in his heart by accumulating material goods, not out of need but only in order to feel secure."

14. "The disease of closed circles, where belonging to a clique becomes more important than belonging to the Body and, in some circumstances, to Christ himself."[62]

How then is this ecclesial culture, so deep-seated in the mind and activity of Christians, so automatic and second nature, to be overcome? Can we accept that there are Catholicisms existing alongside one another, but that not all are Christian, that not all are in tune with the praxis of Jesus or with his spirit, but rather with doctrines, disciplinary forms, and doctrinal interpretations of third parties? Many Christians live an ideologized religion, devoid of faith, without grasping the constitutive dimension comprised of the personal relationships in which we live all and exist. They live a religion without Gospel, or a Christianity without Jesus, because they have never read the gospels nor do they regard them as bedside books for discerning their own ways of life. Ultimately this is about rehumanizing our styles of life, understanding that we are and we make ourselves on the basis of the (social) relations in which we live, evolve, and exist. And to the extent that we render ourselves incapable of establishing such relationships as subjects, of forging permanent kinship bonds with those who are beyond our circle of friends, then we are becoming dehumanized in a slow and asphyxiating process that will rob us of life by emptying it of meaning and transcendence. This nullification of the human in us will result in making us beings of the moment, self-interested, limited to short-term relationships.

While still a cardinal, Bergoglio believed that contemporary society has been rendering itself incapable of establishing genuine community ties despite the technological progress brought by globalization. He used to say that "the whole planet could be connected," but that society is fragmented into diverse interests that have nothing to do with the common good. Hence he proposed as an alternative the way of solidarity in which persons, in the moment of encounter, seek the good of the other and so rehumanize themselves.

This is a humanism that is inscribed in the heart of every human being, like the good Samaritan, who, with no concern for creed or race, picked up an injured stranger, a man whose own people had abused and ignored him. Hence, for Bergoglio, solidarity is the constitutive dimension of the culture of encounter, an element that overcomes the prevailing ecclesial culture, because a person rooted in solidarity "has no right to indifference or to unconcern or to look the other way. We cannot 'keep going,' as the individuals in the parable did. We have a responsibility for the injured . . . , namely the people, which suffers from the fragility of our poorer and more excluded brothers and sisters, the weakness of our institutions, the weakness of our social bonds."[63] This is the Church going out, the church of mercy that wishes to be reconciled with the world, to reencounter itself with the other, its brother and sister, to learn to journey together.

The basis for this model is not found in any ideology or new ecclesiology but in the praxis of Jesus, in the kerygmatic Christology that Francis is describes each day in his homilies. Daily discernment of the Gospel, in contemplation of what it means in terms of action, is what can lead to real change in the ecclesial mindset and begin a process of conversion and return to Jesus. It is out of daily and personal relationship with him that an alternative life can emerge.

A Humanity in the Manner of Jesus: A New Paradigm

The crisis of our time, the crisis of our inability to function as free subjects, to form permanent bonds with others, has had the effect of turning us into indolent creatures, incapable of being affected—appalled—by the fact that people are being crucified in our own day. We have been reduced to living small lives, cocooned with religious elites who no longer know how to connect with the sociocultural reality of the poor majorities.[1] This can be overcome only by an alternative paradigm of humanity, specifically one that is critical of the current ecclesial culture and its emphasis on pastoral self-preservation.[2] The challenge is not to reinvent Christian life, or to create new styles of ecclesial life, but to recover its center, its *essence*, through the historical praxis of Jesus as paradigm of humanity.

The kerygmatic Christology of Francis is faithful to the council spirit as it was received in Latin America, granting primacy to following the Jesus of the gospels, the source of humanization and the hermeneutic criterion for our daily discernment. The pope follows the Christology of *Gaudium et Spes*,[3] which proposes the figure of Jesus as model of humanity, that is, as perfect human being and new human being, one who works for the humanization of every oppressive relationship through true reconciliation. This model of humanity is revealed concretely in Jesus as originating event and archetype of every authentically human way of being. It is a totally inclusive humanity, one that recognizes in every human being a brother or a sister.

What is revealed in the praxis of Jesus that allows him to serve as the paradigm of humankind? The life of Jesus was characterized by a heart open to others, by a yearning for peace and justice. His words and deeds made possible new spaces for re-encountering the other, because he understood that only out of humanizing, inclusive relationships can sin and any distortion of our bonds with our neighbor be halted. This is the message of the good news of the Kingdom. If it is possible to live in the manner that Jesus lived, we can say that injustice and violence will not have the last word, that slavery and death will not put an end to the possibilities of life, that hatred and division are not strong enough to constrain the desires for true human reconciliation in history. Jesus attracts because he was capable of living in solidarity with human persons, restoring to them their dignity, treating them with absolute respect, offering them the good news of a genuine, viable, free, restorative salvation that is not based on the previous moral condition of the individual.

But it is likewise a humanity in process, one that finds its power and meaning in the saving action of compassion. The humanity of Jesus is a humanity that heals the blind (Mt 20:34) and those suffering disease (Mt 9:35); that is pained by the hunger endured by others (Mt 15:32; Mk 8:2–3); that is familiar with the weariness and exhaustion (Mt 9:36) of those whom he encounters on the road, because he also endures these things; that weeps for his friends (Jn 11:35). He rejects war and the violence of Davidic messianism (Lk 19:42; Mk

8:27–38). He offers consolation to widows, the women most
loved and cared for by God (1 Kgs 17:17–24; 2 Kgs 4:32–27;
Sir 4:10; Ps 68:6) because they are among the most forgotten
by society and the religious system (Lk 7:2-15; Lk 18:1–8).
His is a humanity that is learning to bear the life of the other,
that offers the miracle of free self-giving of oneself so that
the other may have primacy and worth: "Come to me, all you
that are weary and are carrying heavy burdens, and I will give
you rest. Take my yoke upon you, and learn from me; for I
am gentle and humble in heart, and you will find rest for
your souls. For my yoke is easy, and my burden is light" (Mt
11:8–29). He is someone who does not regard anyone as lost,
because "if we are faithless, he remains faithful—for he cannot deny himself" (2 Tim 2:13), nor can he betray the truth
that he has preached with his own life.

Hence, knowing Jesus, following him, does not mean
simply professing him, or offering him sacrifices or devotional practices (Ps 50:8–19), but doing today the equivalent
of what he did in his life. This is what it means to live with
the spirit of Jesus as it was transmitted to us by the early
Christian communities. For Pope Francis, it may be the key
element, the criterion of discernment, of genuine commitment in faith, because it is in this world that eternity plays itself out:

> "Come, you that are blessed by my Father, inherit
> the kingdom prepared for you from the foundation
> of the world; for I was hungry and you gave me food,
> I was thirsty and you gave me something to drink, I
> was a stranger and you welcomed me, I was naked
> and you gave me clothing, I was sick and you took
> care of me, I was in prison and you visited me." Then
> the righteous will answer him, "Lord, when was it

that we saw you hungry and gave you food, or thirsty and gave you something to drink? And when was it that we saw you a stranger and welcomed you, or naked and gave you clothing? And when was it that we saw you sick or in prison and visited you?" And the king will answer them, "Truly I tell you, just as you did it to one of the least of these who are members of my family, you did it to me." Then he will say to those at his left hand, "You that are accursed, depart from me into the eternal fire prepared for the devil and his angels; for I was hungry and you gave me no food, I was thirsty and you gave me nothing to drink, I was a stranger and you did not welcome me, naked and you did not give me clothing, sick and in prison and you did not visit me." Then they also will answer, "Lord, when was it that we saw you hungry or thirsty or a stranger or naked or sick or in prison, and did not take care of you?' Then he will answer them, "Truly I tell you, just as you did not do it to one of the least of these, you did not do it to me." And these will go away into eternal punishment, but the righteous into eternal life." (Mt 25: 34–46).

This is not about seeing God in the face of the other, in a form of pantheist piety, let alone through the prism of an ecclesial culture, but of practicing a way of life in which love of God (Dt 6:5) and love of the other (Lev 19:18) have the same weight, that of absolute trust in God the Father (Jn 14:31), and by reason of that love being willing to give one's life for one's friends (Jn 15:13). Indeed, for Jesus there is no love for God that does not likewise entail love for the other, the poorest and most forgotten, the victim, the outcast. "Whoever says, 'I have come to know him' but does not obey his commandments is a liar, and in such a person the truth does not exist" (1 Jn 2:4). Indeed, "If a brother or sister is naked and lacks daily food, and one of you says to them, 'Go in peace; keep warm and eat your fill,' and yet you do not supply their bodily needs, what is the good of that? So faith by itself, if it has no works, is dead." (James 2:15–17). This is the human paradigm on which our following of Jesus must be based,[4] because, "the proposal offered by Jesus is a concrete one and not a notion. It is concrete: 'Go and do the same,' he says to the man who asked 'Who is my neighbor?' After having told the parable of the Good Samaritan, Jesus says, 'Go and do the same.' Nor is this proposal of Jesus...the religiosity of the 'elite.'"[5]

Following Jesus will lead us to discover that we do not approach the poor as social workers or as pastoral agents who are going to give them what they do not have. We go to them because they are the flesh of Christ, and hence we listen to them as to Christ, we treat them as Christ, and we learn from what they tell us as though we were listening to Christ himself.

I would like to conclude with this text, which invites us to reflect on how we incarnate our following of Jesus, who— by surrendering himself to enter into our reality and becoming one in solidarity with us—showed us what it means to be truly human: to surrender self, to enter into the reality of the other, and so, in solidarity with our brothers and sisters, to achieve the fullness of humanity.

> To really help people, the first thing is for us to be truly concerned for individual persons, and I'm thinking of the poor here, valuing them for their goodness. Valuing them, however, also means being ready to learn from them. The poor have much to

teach us about humanity, goodness, sacrifice, and solidarity. As Christians, moreover, we have an additional reason to love and serve the poor; for in them we see the face and the flesh of Christ, who made himself poor so to enrich us with his poverty (cf. 2 Cor 8:9). The poor are the flesh of Christ. When people come to me to confession—and I have fewer opportunities to hear confessions than when I was in the diocese——like to ask them: "Do you help people?" "Yes, I give alms to the poor." "I see, and tell me, when you give alms, do you touch the hand of the person you're giving alms to or do you throw the money to them?" We are speaking of attitudes here. "When you offer alms, do you look into their eyes or do you look the other way?" This demeans the poor person. They are poor. Let us reflect carefully. The poor person is just like me and, if he or she is going through a difficult time for many reasons, whether economic, political, social or personal, it could be me in their place, me longing for someone to help me. As well as desiring this help, if I am in their shoes, I have the right to be respected. We must respect the poor. We must not use the poor person merely as an instrument to placate our guilt. To learn from the poor, with all the realities they experience, all of the values they hold. This is the inspiration for Christians, that the poor are the flesh of Jesus.[6]

ABBREVIATIONS

AG   *Ad Gentes*, Vatican II Decree on the Mission Activity of the Church

Aparecida Fifth General Conference of the Bishops of Latin America and the Caribbean (CELAM V), Aparecida, Brazil, 2007

Aparecida *Aparecida Concluding Document*, Aparecida, Brazil, 2007

CELAM Latin American Episcopal Conference

CELAM II Second General Conference of Latin American Bishops, Medellín, Colombia, 1968

CELAM III Third General Conference of Latin American Bishops, Puebla, Mexico, 1979

CELAM V Fifth General Conference of the Bishops of Latin America and the Caribbean, Aparecida, 2007

COEPAL Argentine Bishops Pastoral Commission

DH   *Dignitatis Humanae*, Vatican II Declaration on Religious Freedom

DM   *Dives in Misericordia*, Pope John Paul II, Encyclical, 1980

EG	*Evangelii Gaudium*, Pope Francis, Apostolic Exhortation, 2013
EN	*Evangelii Nuntiandi*, Pope Paul VI, Apostolic Exhortation, 1975
GS	*Gaudium et Spes*, Vatican II Pastoral Constitution on the Church in the Modern World
LF	*Lumen Fidei*, Pope Francis, Encyclical, 2013
LG	*Lumen Gentium*, Vatican II Dogmatic Constitution on the Church
Medellín	Second General Conference of Latin American Bishops (CELAM II), Medellín, Colombia, 1968
Medellín	*Medellín Final Document*, Medellín, Colombia, 1968
Puebla	Third General Conference of Latin American Bishops (CELAM III), Puebla, Mexico, 1979
Puebla	*Puebla Final Document*, Puebla, Mexico, 1979
SRS	*Sollicitudo Rei Socialis*, Pope John Paul II, Encyclical, 1987

NOTES

INTRODUCTION

1. J. M. Bergoglio, Letter to Catechists in Buenos Aires, August 21, 2008. See also J. M. Bergoglio, "The Message of *Aparecida* to Priests," Brochero, September 11, 2008.

2. Cf. C. Galli, "Teología de la liberación y Doctrina Social de la Iglesia hoy," *Stromata* 46 (1990): 187–203.

3. Cf. R. Antoncich, J. M. Munárriz, *La doctrina Social de la Iglesia* (Madrid: Paulinas, 1987), 13–16.

4. Pope Francis, interview with the editor of *Civiltá Cattolica*, August 19, 2013. Also in *America*, September 30, 2013.

5. Ibid.

6. J. M. Bergoglio, Words at the Meeting of the Priests' Council, Buenos Aires, April 15, 2008.

7. Bergoglio, "The Message of *Aparecida* to Priests."

8. Pope Francis, Address to the Community of the Pontifical Gregorian University, together with Members of the Pontifical Biblical Institute and the Pontifical Oriental Institute, April 10, 2014.

9. J. M. Bergoglio, "Popular Religiosity as Inculturation of the Faith," homily, January 2008.

10. J. M. Bergoglio, *Ponerse la patria al hombro* (Buenos Aires: Claretiana, 2005).

11. J. M. Bergoglio, "Initial Words of the Archbishop at the First Regional Congress on Urban Ministry," homily, August 25, 2011.

12. P. Trigo, "La teología latinoamericana ante los retos epocales." http://gumilla.org/teologialat#.

13. J. C. Scannone, "'Axial Shift' instead of 'Paradigm Shift,'" in *Liberation Theologies on Shifting Grounds. A Clash of Socio-economic and Cultural Paradigms*, ed. G. deSchreijver (Leuven: Peters, 1998).

1. Theology and the People

1. For further information on COEPAL, see S. Politi, *Teología del pueblo: Una propuesta argentina a la teología latinoamericana 1967–1975* (Buenos Aires: Castañeda, 1992), chap. 4; also M. González, *Reflexión teológica en Argentina (1962–2004): Aportes para un mapa de sus relaciones y desafíos hacia el futuro* (Córdoba, Argentina: Docencia, 2005), chap. 2.

2. Other members were Justino O'Farrell, Guillermo Sáenz, Gerardo Farrell, Juan Bautista Capellaro, Fernando Boasso, SJ, Mateo Perdía, Sr. Aída López, Sr. Laura Renard, and Sr. Esther Sastre.

3. *Pastoral Declaration of the Bishops of Argentina: "The Church in the Post-Council Period,"* May 13, 1966.

4. *Medellín Document*, Introduction, 4–5.

5. *Pastoral Declaration of the Bishops of Argentina.*

6. "The circumstances of the life today have been so profoundly changed in their social and cultural aspects that we can speak of a new age of human history. New ways are open, therefore, for the perfection and the further extension of culture. These ways have been prepared by the enormous growth of natural, human, and social sciences, by technical progress, and by advances in developing and organizing media of communication. Hence the culture of today possesses particular characteristics: sciences that are called exact greatly develop critical judgment; the more recent psychological studies more profoundly explain human activity; historical studies make it much easier to see things in terms of change and evolution; customs and patterns of living are becoming more and more uniform; industrialization, urbanization, and other causes that promote community living create a mass culture from which are born new ways of thinking, acting, and making use of leisure. The increase of commerce between the various nations and human groups opens the treasures of different civilizations to all and thus, little by little, there develops a more universal form of human culture, one which better promotes and expresses the unity of the human race to the degree that it preserves the particular aspects of the different civilizations" (*GS* 54).

7. *Gaudium et Spes* 55.

8. *Gaudium et Spes* 57.

9. *Pastoral Declaration of the Argentine Bishops "The Church in the Post-council Period."*

10. L. Gera, "Reflexiones teológicas sobre la Iglesia," in *Escritos teológico-pastorales de Lucio Gera. I: Del preconcilio a la Conferencia de Puebla (1956–1981)*, ed. V. Azcuy, C. Galli, and M. González (Buenos Aires: Ágape, 2006), 358.

11. *Lumen Gentium* 13.

12. Gera, "Reflexiones teológicas sobre la Iglesia," 358.

13. *Evangelii Gaudium* 114.

14. God "does not make men and women holy and save them merely as individuals, without bond or link with one another. Rather, he wishes to bring them together as one people..., He therefore chose the people of Israel to be his own people. With them he set up a covenant. Step by step he taught and prepared this people, making known in the course of their history both himself and his intentions" (*LG* 9).

15. *Evangelii Gaudium* 113.

16. R. Tello, "Nota (e). Cultura y pueblo," in *Pueblo y cultura I* (Buenos Aires: Patria Grande, 2011), 194.

17. Cf. S. Politi, *Teología del pueblo: una propuesta argentina a la teología latinoamericana, 1967–1975* (San Antonio de Padua—Buenos Aires: Ediciones Castañeda—Editorial Guadalupe, 1992).

18. Gera participated not only in Medellín as a *peritus* but also in Puebla, and he became a member of the CELAM theologico-pastoral team and of the International Theological Commission. Many regard him as the most important Argentine theologian of the second half of the twentieth century.

19. R. Tello, *Reunión de los peritos de la Coepal, 30 de marzo de 1969* (Ediciones Volveré, Fascículo 5, 2015).

20. Ibid.

21. Conference of Bishops of Argentina, *San Miguel Document* (Conferencia Episcopal Argentina, *Documento de San Miguel, Declaración del Episcopado Argentino sobre la adaptación a la realidad actual del país de las Conclusiones de la II Conferencia General del Episcopado Latinoamericano [Medellín]*). 1969. Chapter 6: Popular Ministry, 4.

22. Ibid., 5.

23. "The people do not have a uniform movement; on the contrary, they travel somewhat diverging routes, suffer alien influences, have periods of latency, of calm, at least apparently, in which it is difficult to recognize it and interpret it." R. Tello, *Fundamentos de una nueva evangelización II*, Observación 46. (Unpublished).

24. R. Tello, *Fundamentos de una nueva evangelización* (Buenos Aires: Patria Grande-Ágape, 2015), 234.

25. Cf. O. C. Albado, "¿Y el pueblo dónde está? Reflexiones en torno a la importancia del pueblo en Rafael Tello," in *Vida Pastoral* 320 (2013): 4–9.

26. P. Rodari, "Conversaciones con Víctor Manuel Fernández," *Iglesia Viva* 259 (July–September, 2014): 65.

27. Bolivia, August 7, 2015.

28. *Evangelii Gaudium* 241.

29. R. Tello, "Nueva evangelización. Anexo I," *Escritos teológico-pastorales de Lucio Gera. I: Del preconcilio a la Conferencia de Puebla (1956–1981)*, ed. V. Azcuy, C. Galli, and M. González (Buenos Aires: Ágape, 2006), 486.

30. Gera, "Reflexiones teológicas sobre la Iglesia," 363.

31. "What is most characteristic of the hope of the poor is that it comes out experiencing limits and is nourished by that experience. That is why it is hope in the theological sense of the word. Poverty is turned into a stance of hope. Lack of goods presents the negative side of poverty; the positive side of poverty is hope. The poor are not merely those who hope because 'everything's going fine for them,' but those who hope 'despite everything,' all the negative going on in this world." L. Gera, "Entrevista al cumplir sus 50 anos de sacerdocio," en *Ministerio peregrino y mendicante. Lucio Gera 50, años de sacerdocio*, ed. V. R. Azcuy, P. Scervino. In *Nuevo Mundo* 55 (1998): 51–52.

32. "The Proposal for an 'Argentine Medellín,' has reached its proper expression: popular ministry, which is simply placing the Church at the service of the popular expression of Christian life. Not only valuing popular religiosity, which comes from a narrow and theologically ambiguous perspective, but favoring the popular expression of Christianity, understood as Christian life... Popular Christianity is much more than popular religiosity, with its own way of living the theological virtues, which are the heart of Christian life." F. Forcat, "En las nacientes de la pastoral popular," *Stromata* 71 (2015): 155.

33. R. Tello, "Algo más acerca del pueblo," in *Pueblo y cultura* 1, (Buenos Aires: Patria Grande, 2011), 15.

34. Tello, *Nueva evangelización. Anexo I*, 486.

35. *Evangelii Gaudium* 125.

36. V. M. Fernández, "El *sensus populi*: la legitimidad de una teología desde el pueblo," *Teología* 72 (1998): 139.

37. C. Galli, "Evangelización, cultura y teología: El aporte de J. C. Scannone a una teología inculturada," *Teología* 58 (1991): 195.

38. J. C. Scannone, "La teología de la liberación," *Concilium* 93 (1974): 467.

39. J. M. Bergoglio, *Te Deum* held in the cathedral of Buenos Aires, May 25, 2003.

40. P. Trigo, "Teología de la liberación y cultura," *Revista Latinoamericana de Teología* 4 (1985): 89.

41. L. Gera, "Pueblo, religión del pueblo e Iglesia," a presentation given at a meeting on Popular Religiosity in Latin America, August 26, 1976, Bogotá, and published in *Iglesia y religiosidad popular en América*

Latina (Bogotá: CELAM, 1977). It appears in *Escritos teológico-pastorales de Lucio Gera*, 730–31.

42. Fernández, "El *sensus populi*," 162.

43. Cf. J. C. Scannone, "La teología argentina del pueblo," in *Gregorianum* 96 (2015): 12–13.

44. I. A. Fresia, "Teología del pueblo, de la cultura y de la pastoral popular," *Stromata* 70 (2014): 230.

45. The text continues: "[One can also note] a habit which for the sophisticated and those who have economic power may be considered a defect or a vice. It is what Saint Thomas calls *gnome*, and he describes it as follows: 'Sometimes it happens that something must be done outside the usual rules, as for example, not returning a deposit to someone who is going to use it against the nation or other things like that; and these things must be judged according to principles higher than the common ones' (*STh* 51,4). Tello also mentions other considerations from Cajetan, considerations emphasizing that the clear-sightedness found in many simple people, who are rich in natural wisdom, enables them to discern beyond the law, a skill often not found in the more highly educated. Thus, Tello suggests recognizing that 'ordinary people are especially astute, as a result of a long experience in history, for safeguarding certain values' (*NEI*, 51)." V. M. Fernández, "Con los pobres hasta el fondo: el pensamiento teológico de Rafael Tello," *Revista Proyecto* 36 (2000): 201.

46. P. Trigo, "Teología de la liberación y cultura," *Revista Latinoamericana de Teología* 4 (1985): 90–91.

47. Rodari, "Conversaciones con Víctor Manuel Fernández," 65.

48. J. O'Farrell, *América Latina: ¿cuáles son tus problemas?* (Buenos Aires: Editora Patria Grande, 1976), 17.

49. Pope Francis, Address to the Joint Session of the United States Congress, Washington, DC, September 24, 2015.

50. "In his vision, the people is an agent in history made up of concrete persons, each of whom should have his or her voice in the dialogue to work out a project of common life, of integral development. Bergoglio seeks to get away from formal abstract visions, from plans written down on paper without taking into account the reality in which they are to be applied. The connection to reality, with concrete human beings, is key to his thinking and evident in his words and in his acts, as, for example, when he speaks of looking at the poor person, the elderly person, the person with a disability in the eye, and using the Good Samaritan as an example. Or when he refers to the teachings of St. Ignatius, highlighting the spirit of discernment, the need to listen for the precise life circumstance of a person or a community before making a decision that affects him or it." B. Díaz, "Alberto Methol Ferré: una in-

fluencia fundamental en el pensamiento del Papa Francisco," *Cuadernos del Claeh* 101 (2015): 67.

51. To delve more deeply into this, see G. DeSchrijver, "Paradigm Shift in Third-World Theologies of Liberation: From Socio-economic Analysis to Cultural Analysis?" in *Liberation Theologies on Shifting Grounds: A Clash of Socio-economic and Cultural Paradigms*, ed. G. De-Schrijver (Leuven: Peeters, 1998).

52. Tello, *Reunión de los peritos de la Coepal, 30 de marzo de 1969*.

53. Pope Francis, Meeting with Clergy, Religious, and Seminarians at the National Marian Shrine of "El Quinche," Quito, Ecuador, July 8, 2015.

54. Pope Francis, Speech at the Meeting with Priests, Religious, and Seminarians at the Stadium of Don Bosco School, Santa Cruz, Bolivia, Thursday, July 9, 2015.

55. J. M. Bergoglio, *Ponerse la patria al hombre* (Buenos Aires: Claretiana, 2005), 6. These words were spoken at the *Te Deum* held in the cathedral in Buenos Aires on May 25, 1999.

56. Tello, *Nueva evangelización. Anexo I*, 52–54, cited in the article of V. M. Fernández, "Con los pobres hasta el fondo: el pensamiento teológico de Rafael Tello," in *Revista Proyecto* 36 (2000): 204.

57. Pope Francis, Video Message to Participants in an International Theological Congress Held at the Pontifical Catholic University of Argentina, Buenos Aires, September 1–3, 2015.

58. J. M. Bergoglio, *Te Deum* held in the cathedral of Buenos Aires, May 25, 2000.

59. J. C. Scannone, "La globalización como hecho e ideología," in *Argentina: alternativas frente a la globalización* (Buenos Aires: San Pablo, 1999), 253–90.

60. P. Ricoeur, "Universal Civilization and National Cultures," in *History and Truth* (Evanston, IL: Northwestern University Press, 1965), originally in *Esprit* (1961) 29/10.

61. Ibid.

62. "An innate tension also exists between globalization and localization. We need to pay attention to the global so as to avoid narrowness and banality. Yet we also need to look to the local, which keeps our feet on the ground. Together, the two prevent us from falling into one of two extremes. In the first, people get caught up in an abstract, globalized universe, falling into step behind everyone else, admiring the glitter of other people's worlds, gaping and applauding at all the right times. At the other extreme, they turn into a museum of local folklore, a world apart, doomed to doing the same things over and over and incapable of being challenged by novelty or appreciating the beauty that God bestows beyond their borders" (*EG* 234).

63. "Peace is founded not only on respect for human rights but also on respect for the rights of peoples, in particular the right to independence" (Pontifical Council for Justice and Peace, *Compendium of the Social Doctrine of the Church*, 157). Pope Francis, Address to the Second World Meeting of Popular Movements, Bolivia, July 9, 2015.

64. L. Gera, "Puebla: evangelización de la cultura," *Teología* 33 (1979): 76.

65. Ibid., 75.

66. *Gaudium et Spes* 60.

67. "The word 'culture' in its general sense indicates everything whereby man develops and perfects his many bodily and spiritual qualities; he strives by his knowledge and his labor to bring the world itself under his control. He renders social life more human both in the family and the civic community, through improvement of customs and institutions. Throughout the course of time he expresses, communicates, and conserves in his works, great spiritual experiences and desires, that they might be of advantage to the progress of many, even of the whole human family. Thence it follows that human culture has necessarily a historical and social aspect and the word 'culture' also often assumes a sociological and ethnological sense. According to this sense we speak of a plurality of cultures. Different styles of life and multiple scales of values arise from the diverse manner of using things, of laboring, of expressing oneself, of practicing religion, of forming customs, of establishing laws and juridic institutions, of cultivating the sciences, the arts, and beauty. Thus the customs handed down to it form the patrimony proper to each human community. It is also in this way that there is formed the definite, historical milieu that enfolds the man of every nation and age and from which he draws the values which permit him to promote civilization" (*GS* 53).

68. "From day to day, in every group or nation, there is an increase in the number of men and women who are conscious that they themselves are the authors and the artisans of the culture of their community. Throughout the whole world there is a mounting increase in the sense of autonomy as well as of responsibility. This is of paramount importance for the spiritual and moral maturity of the human race. This becomes clearer if we consider the unification of the world and the duty which is imposed upon us, that we build a better world based upon truth and justice. Thus we are witnesses of the birth of a new humanism, one in which people are defined first of all by their responsibility to their brothers and sisters and to history" (*GS* 55).

69. *Gaudium et Spes* 53.

70. Gera, "Puebla: evangelización de la cultura," 78.

71. Ibid., 80.

72. "Culture is a 'preference,' a hierarchy of values: a hierarchy more actually lived than established theoretically. It is a 'style.' Style is a certain way of shaping life." Ibid., 79.

73. A. N'Daw, "Universal Culture and National Cultures," in *Cultural Rights as Human Rights* (Paris: UNESCO, 1970), 28–30.

74. Ibid.

75. UNESCO, Universal Declaration on Cultural Diversity, November 2, 2001, art. 7.

76. N'Daw, "Universal Culture and National Cultures," 32.

77. Ibid., 12.

78. Ricoeur, "Universal Civilization and National Cultures," 283.

79. Cf. Pope John Paul II, *Ecclesia in America*, 20.

80. Pope John Paul II, Address of the Holy Father to the Pontifical Academic of Social Sciences, April 27, 2001, in *L'Osservatore Romano*, May 11, 2001, 4.

81. Pope John Paul II, *Ecclesia in America*, 55.

82. *Evangelii Gaudium* 54.

2. Responding to the New Signs of the Times

1. Z. Bauman, *Globalization: The Human Consequences* (New York: Columbia University Press, 1998), 60.

2. Ibid., 59.

3. *Aparecida* 90.

4. Among other works, the following may be consulted: G. Lipovetsky, *Hypermodern Times* (Cambridge: Polity, 2005), and *La sociedad de la decepción* (Barcelona: Anagrama, 2006).

5. Cf. M. Weber, *Economy and Society.* (Berkeley: University of California Press, 1978).

6. *Evangelii Gaudium* 62.

7. *Aparecida* 46.

8. J. M. Bergoglio, *Carta al inicio de la Cuaresma*, Buenos Aires 2013.

9. "We have created new idols. The worship of the ancient golden calf (cf. Ex 32:1–35) has returned in a new and ruthless guise in the idolatry of money and the dictatorship of an impersonal economy lacking a truly human purpose. The worldwide crisis affecting finance and the economy lays bare their imbalances and, above all, their lack of real concern for human beings; man is reduced to one of his needs alone: consumption" (*EG* 55).

10. This can happen for two reasons: "Either for lack of human development, for scarce development of their capacities; or for the structural reason which is at the basis of the dialectical notion of poverty: the property structure and the productive and sociopolitical structure prevent the poor as a social totality from getting out of poverty, even though they hard and well." P. Trigo, *Echar la suerte con los pobres de la tierra* (Caracas: Centro Gumilla, 2015), 11.

11. "And if the dynamic of the established or prevailing order continues, the result will be a world situation more inhumane than any in our history." Ibid., 12.

12. Francis, Apostolic visit to Cagliari. Meeting with Workers, September 22, 2013.

13. "Just as the commandment 'Thou shalt not kill' sets a clear limit in order to safeguard the value of human life, today we also have to say 'thou shalt not' to an economy of exclusion and inequality. Such an economy kills. How can it be that it is not a news item when an elderly homeless person dies of exposure, but it is news when the stock market loses two points? This is a case of exclusion. Can we continue to stand by when food is thrown away while people are starving? This is a case of inequality. Today everything comes under the laws of competition and the survival of the fittest, where the powerful feed upon the powerless. As a consequence, masses of people find themselves excluded and marginalized: without work, without possibilities, without any means of escape. Human beings are themselves considered consumer goods to be used and then discarded. We have created a 'throwaway' culture which is now spreading. It is no longer simply about exploitation and oppression, but something new. Exclusion ultimately has to do with what it means to be a part of the society in which we live; those excluded are no longer society's underside or its fringes or its disenfranchised—they are no longer even a part of it. The excluded are not the 'exploited' but the outcast, the 'leftovers'" (*EG* 53).

14. Z. Bauman, *Wasted Lives: Modernity and Its Outcasts* (Cambridge: Polity, 2004), 132.

15. "The trap of impotence leads us to think: does it make sense to try to change all this? Can we do something about this situation? Is it worthwhile attempting it if the world continues its carnival-like dance, disguising everything for a while?" J. M. Bergoglio, Letter at the beginning of Lent, 2013.

16. Bauman describes the psychosocial effect of this situation very well: "Faced with the daunting task of gaining the means of biological survival while stripped of the self-confidence and self-esteem needed to sustain their social survival, they have no reason to contemplate and

savor the subtle distinctions between suffering by design and misery by default…Whether by explicit or by an implied though never officially published verdict, they have become superfluous, unnecessary, unneeded and unwanted, and their reactions, off the mark or absent, render the censure a self-fulfilling prophecy" (*Wasted Lives*, 40).

17. "'Adam, where are you?' This is the first question that God addresses to man after his sin. 'Where are you Adam?' Adam is disoriented and has lost his place in creation because he thought to become powerful, to dominate everything, to be God. And harmony was broken, the man erred—and this is repeated even in relations with his neighbor, who is no longer a brother to be loved, but simply someone who disturbs my life, my well-being." Pope Francis, Apostolic visit to Lampedusa. Arenas Athletic Field, July 8, 2013.

18. "And God puts the second question: 'Cain, where is your brother?' The dream of being powerful, of being as great as God, even of being God, leads to a chain of errors that is a chain of death, leads to shedding the blood of the brother!" Ibid.

19. "The option for the poor is on behalf of those persons who are poor, so that they cease to be so. Hence we have insisted that, in itself, this option has no place in the established order, which is what manufactures them structurally as a necessary consequence of policies that favor those on top, and hence it constitutes a subversive force. The established order strives to claim that the existence of poor people is only an undesired collateral effect, for which it is not responsible, because it seeks only the end that it directly pursues and for which it accepts no responsibility. But it is obvious that this reasoning is not solid, but rather the expression of a dehumanizing irresponsibility." Trigo, *Echar la suerte con los pobres de la tierra*, 101–102.

20. *Evangelii Gaudium* 202.

21. P. Trigo, "La cultura en los barrios," *Revista SIC* 507 (1988): 294.

22. L. Gera, "Reflexiones teológicas sobre la Iglesia," in *Escritos teológico-pastorales de Lucio Gera. I: Del preconcilio a la Conferencia de Puebla (1956–1981)*, ed. V. Azcuy, C. Galli, and M. González (Buenos Aires: Ágape, 2006), 356.

23. Ibid.

24. "Where underdeveloped countries are concerned, the Church presents itself as it is and as it wants to be, as Church of all, and especially as the Church of the poor. Any offense against and violation of the fifth and sixth commandments of the sacred Decalogue; any disregard of the commitments that follow from the seventh commandment; the miseries of life in society that call for vengeance in the sight of God; all of these must be recalled and deplored. It is duty of all human beings, and even

more for of Christians, to consider the superfluous in light of the needs of the neighbor and to see to it that the management and distribution of created goods be done to the advantage of all. This is what it means to spread the social and community sense that is innate in authentic Christianity: all of this is to be vigorously affirmed." Radio address of Pope John XXIII, September 11, 1962.

25. *Medellín* 5, 15.

26. "We remind you of what was said by a great and wise bishop, Bossuet, on the 'eminent dignity of the poor' (Cf. J.-B. Bossuet *De l'eminente dignite des Pauvres*). The entire tradition of the churches recognizes in the poor the sacrament of Christ, certainly not identical to the reality of the Eucharist, but indeed in perfect analogical and mystical correspondence with it." Paul VI, Apostolic pilgrimage to Bogota on the occasion of the 39th International Eucharistic Congress; homily during the Mass for Colombian peasants, August 23, 1968.

27. Cf. *Document of the Pact of the Catacombs*, signed on November 16, 1965, in the catacomb of Saint Domitila in Rome, 2–3.

28. Ibid., 1.

29. "Conscious of the requirements of justice and charity and of their mutual relatedness, we will seek to transform our works of welfare into social works based on charity and justice, so that they take all persons into account, as a humble service to the responsible public agencies. See Matthew 25:31–46; Luke 13:12–14; 13:33–34." Ibid., 10.

30. Thus, the bishops say that they will "request jointly, at the level of international organizations, the adoption of economic and cultural structures which, instead of producing poor nations in an ever richer world, make it possible for the poor majorities to free themselves from their wretchedness. We will do all this even as we bear witness to the gospel, after the example of Pope Paul VI at the United Nations." Ibid., 11.

31. Ibid.

32. Conference of Bishops of Argentina, *San Miguel Document* (Conferencia Episcopal Argentina, *Documento de San Miguel, Declaración del Episcopado Argentino sobre la adaptación a la realidad actual del país de las Conclusiones de la II Conferencia General del Episcopado Latinoamericano [Medellín]*). 1969. Part III: "Poverty of the Church."

33. Trigo, *Echar la suerte con los pobres de la tierra*, 42.

34. "In the exhortation *Evangelii Gaudium* we find harmony with the main categories of liberation theologies and it colors the entire document." G. Villagrán Medina, "La dimensión social de *Evangelii Gaudium*," *Proyección* 61 (2014): 181.

35. Title used to refer to Jesus twice in the *San Miguel Document*, Part III, "Poverty of the Church."

36. *San Miguel Document*, Part III, "Poverty of the Church."

37. "Christ, our Savior, not only loved the poor, but rather, 'being rich he became poor,' he lived in poverty. His mission centered on advising the poor of their liberation and he founded the Church as the sign of that poverty among men." *Medellín*, "Poverty of the Church," 7.

38. *Medellín*, "Introduction to the Conclusions," 6.

39. "The poor merit preferential attention, whatever the moral or personal situation in which they find themselves" (*Puebla* 1142).

40. "The *ubi* must be permeated with the *quid*. Wherever it may be done empirically, theology has to let itself be deeply affected by the reality of the poor. It is their suffering that must prompt thinking, it is their hope that has to give shape to the salvific bent of all Christian theology. In other words, theology can be done in many physical places, but it has to be done from the reality of the poor." J. Sobrino, "Los signos de los tiempos en la teología de la liberación," in J. M. Lera (ed.), *Fides quae per caritatem operatur. Homenaje a Juan Alfaro SJ en su 75 cumpleaños.* (Bilbao: Universidad Deusto—Ediciones Mensajero, 1989), 262.

41. There are many people who do not think that the cause of the poor is their problem. "We do not hear them, we do not recognize them. Deafness. Here we have the temptation to see suffering as something natural, to take injustice for granted. And yes, there are people like that: I am here with God, with my consecrated life, chosen by God for ministry and yes, it is normal that there are those who are sick, poor, suffering, and it is so normal that I no longer notice the cry for help. To become accustomed. We say to ourselves, 'This is nothing unusual; things were always like this—as long as it does not affect me.' It is the response born of a blind, closed heart, a heart that has lost the ability to be touched and hence the possibility to change. How many of us followers of Christ run the risk of losing our ability to be astonished, even with the Lord?" Pope Francis, Address to Clergy, Religious, and Seminarians in Santa Cruz, Bolivia, July 9, 2015.

42. *Lumen Gentium* 8.

43. Pope Francis, Homily, Quito, July 7, 2015.

44. "The anti-value today, I believe, is human merchandise, in other words, the marketing of persons. Man and woman become one more piece of merchandise among the projects that come to us from somewhere else, that become established in society, and in some fashion go against our human dignity. This is the anti-value: the human person as merchandise in the political, economic, and social system." J. M. Bergoglio, *Fourth Conference on Social Ministry*, Buenos Aires, June 30, 2001.

45. Pope Francis, Address to Representatives of Civil Society, Asunción, Paraguay, July 11, 2015.

46. Pope Francis, Address to the First World Meeting of Popular Movements. Rome, October 28, 2014.

47. A. Spadaro, "Wake Up the World!" Conversation with Pope Francis about the Religious Life," in *La Civiltà Cattolica* I (2014), translated by Fr. Donald Maldari, SJ. http://www.laciviltacattolica.it/articoli_download/extra/Wake_up_the_world.pdf.

48. "Truly to understand reality we need to move away from the central position of calmness and peacefulness and direct ourselves to the peripheral areas. Being at the periphery helps to see and understand better, to analyze reality more correctly, to shun centralism and ideological approaches." Ibid.

49. Ibid., 4.

50. "Without the preferential option for the poor, the proclamation of the Gospel, which is itself the prime form of charity, risks being misunderstood or submerged by the ocean of words" (*EG* 199).

51. "Our commitment does not consist exclusively in activities or programs of promotion and assistance; what the Holy Spirit mobilizes is not an unruly activism, but above all an attentiveness which considers the other 'in a certain sense as one with ourselves.' This loving attentiveness is the beginning of a true concern for their person which inspires me effectively to seek their good." Ibid.

52. Pope Francis, Address to the Second World Meeting of Popular Movements, Bolivia, July 9, 2015.

53. Pope Francis, Address to the First World Meeting of Popular Movements.

54. Pope Francis, Address to the Second World Meeting of Popular Movements.

55. Pope Francis, Address to the First World Meeting of Popular Movements.

56. Ibid.

57. Pope Francis, Address to the Second World Meeting of Popular Movements.

58. Ibid.

59. G. Gutierrez, *Líneas pastorales de la Iglesia en América Latina* (Lima: CEP, 1988), 64. The observations in this book were originally offered in 1968 and first published in 1970.

60. Ibid., 66.

61. "Without truly going to the fringes, . . . good proposals and projects remain stuck in the realm of ideas." Pope Francis, Address to the First World Meeting of Popular Movements.

62. "The condition of salvation is love: salvation is fruit of love; one who loves is saved, that is, one who enters into communion with human

beings enters into communion with God." Gutierrez, *Líneas pastorales de la Iglesia en América Latina*, 65.

63. Pope Francis, Address to the Second World Meeting of Popular Movements.

64. Gera's original text is entitled: "La teología de los procesos históricos," *Revista de Teología* 87 (2005): 259–79. It was later compiled into the publication of his theological-pastoral writings: L. Gera, "Teología de los procesos históricos y de la vida de las personas," in *Escritos teológico-pastorales de Lucio Gera. 2: De la Conferencia de Puebla a nuestros días (1982–2007)*, ed. V. Azcuy, C. Galli, M. González (Buenos Aires: Ágape, 2007), 869–90.

65. "It is a matter of reading an event, a 'fact' of history, as sign, that is of grasping the saving (theological) meaning implicated in this fact or process. Hence events (processes) are discerned or interpreted, 'in the light of the Gospel' (*GS* 4) or 'of the faith... for faith illuminates everything with a new light...' (*GS* 11)." L. Gera, "La teología de los procesos históricos," 270.

66. "I believe that the council Fathers have leaned toward appreciating as preponderant sign of the activity of the Spirit in this age universal brother/sisterhood. In it are involved justice and peace or concord, and beyond them, love: love which, going beyond justice, is expressed as solidarity." Ibid., 269.

67. "The object that is to be known is the fact, the event or historic process as sign." Ibid., 265–69.

68. Pope Francis, Address to the First World Meeting of Popular Movements.

69. Gera, "La teología de los procesos históricos," 265–66.

70. Cf. R. Luciani, "Los signos de los tiempos como criterio hermenéutico fundamental del quehacer teológico," *Atualidade Teologica* 52 (2016): 53–54.

3. TOWARD A LIBERATING PASTORAL MINISTRY
OF PEOPLES AND THEIR CULTURES

1. As Pope Paul VI explains: "Basically, these inquiries make explicit the fundamental question that the Church is asking herself today and which may be expressed in the following terms: after the Council and thanks to the Council... does the Church or does she not find herself better equipped to proclaim the Gospel and to put it into people's hearts with conviction, freedom of spirit and effectiveness?" (*EN* 2–4).

2. R. Tello, *Fundamentos de una Nueva Evangelización* (Buenos Aires: Patria Grande-Ágape, 2015), 42–43.

3. R. Tello, *Pueblo y cultura popular* (Buenos Aires: Ágape, 2014), 233.

4. Pope John Paul II, *Redemptoris Missio* 14. Likewise in *Dives in Misericordia* he stated that the human subject is the way of the Church, and therefore "the more the Church's mission is centered upon man— the more it is, so to speak, anthropocentric—the more it must be confirmed and actualized theocentrically" (*DM* 1).

5. O. C. Albado, "La pastoral popular en el pensamiento del padre Rafael Tello," *Franciscanum* 160 (2013): 226.

6. *Medellín* 1, 10.

7. *Medellín* 2, 15.

8. Cf. *Medellín*, Introduction, 4–5. We should frame the aspirations in the following context being experienced in Latin America, as explained at Medellín in the document on lay movements: "Let us recall that the present historical moment our people are living is characterized in the social order and from an objective point of view by conditions of underdevelopment dramatized by the imposing phenomena of marginality, alienation and poverty, and largely influenced, in the last analysis, by economic, political, and cultural structures dependent on the industrialized metropolises which monopolize technology and science (neo-colonialism). From the subjective point of view it is characterized by the personal awareness of this situation which awakens among large sectors of Latin Americans attitudes of protest and the desire for liberation, development and social justice." *Medellín* 10, 2.

9. *Medellín*, Introduction, 2, 22.

10. *Medellín*, Introduction, 7, 13.

11. "The greatest fruit of the 1968 CELAM Conference was that it gave birth to the Latin American Church as Latin American. The Medellín documents represent the founding act of the Church of Latin America based on and for its peoples and their cultures." C. Boff, "La originalidad histórica de Medellín," in *Revista Electrónica Latinoamericana de Teología*" 203, p. 1. http://www.servicioskoinonia.org/relat/203.htm.

12. "Community life is particularly important for Christians as a testimony of love and unity. Catechesis cannot therefore limit itself to the dimensions of the individual life. Base Christian communities, open to the world and living in it, must be the fruit of evangelization" (*Medellín* 8, 10).

13. E. F. Pironio, "La evangelización del mundo de hoy en América Latina," presentation at the 1974 Synod of Bishops.

14. *Medellín* 15, 10.

15. Conference of Bishops of Argentina, *San Miguel Document* (Conferencia Episcopal Argentina, *Documento de San Miguel, Declaración*

del Episcopado Argentino sobre la adaptación a la realidad actual del país de las Conclusiones de la II Conferencia General del Episcopado Latinoamericano, Medellín. 1969. Justice, 1.2.

16. L. Gera, "Puebla: evangelización de la cultura," *Teología* 33 (1979): 71–89.

17. Ibid., 79.

18. *Medellín*, Introduction, 6.

19. R. Tello, "Evangelización y cultura," in *Pueblo y cultura popular* (Buenos Aires: Patria Grande-Ágape, 2014), 241.

20. *San Miguel Document*, Chapter 6: Popular Ministry, 4.

21. *Medellín* 5.15.

22. *San Miguel Document*, Chapter 3: Poverty of the Church, 2.

23. P. Trigo, "¿Ha muerto la teología de la liberación? La realidad actual y sus causas. Parte I," *Relat* 64 (2005): 58–59.

24. "Listening to the cry of those who suffer violence and are oppressed by unjust systems and structures, and hearing the appeal of a world that by its perversity contradicts the plan of its Creator, we have shared our awareness of the Church's vocation to be present in the heart of the world by proclaiming the Good News to the poor, freedom to the oppressed, and joy to the afflicted." Second General Assembly of the Synod of Bishops, Introduction (1971).

25. "Action on behalf of justice and participation in the transformation of the world fully appear to us as a constitutive dimension of the reaching of the Gospel, or, in other words, of the Church's mission for the redemption of the human race and its liberation from every oppressive situation." Ibid.

26. Cf. Ibid. This was then assumed by Pope John Paul II in *Redemptor Hominis* in the following terms: "In reality, the name for that deep amazement at man's worth and dignity is the Gospel, that is to say: the Good News. It is also called Christianity. This amazement determines the Church's mission in the world and, perhaps even more so, in the modern world" (n. 10).

27. "[I]t is impossible to conceive true progress without recognizing the necessity—within the political system chosen—of a development composed both of economic growth and participation." *Second General Assembly of the Synod of Bishops*, 1971.

28. CELAM, *Evangelización, desafío de la Iglesia. Sínodo de 1974: documentos papales y sinodales. Presencia del CELAM y del Episcopado Latinoamericano.* (Bogotá: CELAM, 1976).

29. "Pironio spoke of "the paschal face of the Church of Latin America, marked by the cross, and hope; the centrality of evangelization; the riches of popular Catholic religiosity; the commitment to integral

liberation; the drive of youth ministry; the novelty of grassroots ecclesial communities; the emergence of new ministries; the treasure of Latin American Marian piety, which he embodied with such great love for the Virgin of Luján and he expressed his famous prayer to Our Lady of America. He said that we were at the beginning of a new evangelization. With this expression, which had appeared in *Medellín* (6, 8), he set forth the need to undertake 'a new stage in evangelization.'" C. Galli, "En la Iglesia sopla un viento del sur," *Teología* 108 (2012): 114.

30. Pironio, "La evangelización del mundo de hoy en América Latina."

31. Ibid.

32. *Medellín* 5, 15.

33. Synod of Bishops, 1974, 71.

34. *Evangelii Nuntiandi*, 29.

35. "Between evangelization and human advancement (development and liberation) there are in fact profound links. These include links of an anthropological order, because the man who is to be evangelized is not an abstract being but is subject to social and economic questions. They also include links in the theological order, since one cannot dissociate the plan of creation from the plan of Redemption. The latter plan touches the very concrete situations of injustice to be combated and of justice to be restored. They include links of the eminently evangelical order, which is that of charity: how in fact can one proclaim the new commandment without promoting in justice and in peace the true, authentic advancement of man?" (*EN* 31).

36. *Evangelii Nuntiandi* 31.

37. *Evangelii Nuntiandi* 28.

38. "As the kernel and center of His Good News, Christ proclaims salvation, this great gift of God which is liberation from everything that oppresses man" (*EN* 9).

39. Paul VI, Speech at the Opening of the Third General Assembly of the Synod of Bishops, September 27, 1974.

40. *Evangelii Gaudium* 113.

41. Cf. L Gera, "Teología de los procesos históricos y de la vida de las personas," in *Escritos teológico-pastorales de Lucio Gera. 2: De la Conferencia de Puebla a nuestros días (1982–2007)*, ed. V. Azcuy, C. Galli, M. González (Buenos Aires: Ágape, 2007), 265–67.

42. B. Kloppenburg, "Evangelización liberadora," in *Medellín* 26 (1981): 233.

43. "Cultures are continually subjected to new developments and to mutual encounter and interpretation. In the course of their history they go through periods in which they are challenged by new values or anti-values,

and by the need to effect new syntheses of their way of life. The Church feels particularly summoned to make its presence felt, to be there with the Gospel, when old ways of social life and value-organization are decaying or dying in order to make new room for syntheses. It is better to evangelize new cultural forms when they are being born than when they are already full-grown and established. This is the global challenge that confronts the Church today because 'we can truly speak of a new age in human history' (*GS* 54). Hence the Latin American Church seeks to give new impetus to the evangelization of our continent." *Puebla* 393.

44. Pope John Paul II, *Speech to the Nineteenth Assembly of CELAM*, Haiti, March 9, 1983, n. 3. Also cited in *Ecclesia in America* 6.

45. *Ecclesia in America* 21, 54, 69.

46. Ibid., 12.

47. Ibid., 18, 67.

48. Ibid., 18.

49. Trigo, "¿Ha muerto la teología de la liberación?" 59.

50. P. Arrupe, *Letter and Document on Inculturation*, 1/5/78, in *Acta Romana Societatis Iesu* XVII (1978), 230. English in Pedro Arrupe, *Other Apostolates Today*, vol. 3 (St. Louis: Institute of Jesuit Sources, 1981), 172.

51. Ibid.

52. "The inculturation of the faith is also a kind of liberation insofar as it helps dislodge, with the values of the Good news, the false values of alien imposed cultures: cultural domination is a form of oppression." Arrupe, *Letter and Document on Inculturation*, 245 (n. 30).

53. As Francis warns: "we in the Church can sometimes fall into a needless hallowing of our own culture, and thus show more fanaticism than true evangelizing zeal" (*EG* 117).

54. "The Gospel and hence evangelization are not identified with any culture but they are not incompatible with them; they are capable of penetrating all without being subject to any. They do this, according to the document of the 1974 Synod, in a new and exclusive way: by preaching the need of personal conversion, the violence of the Kingdom, charity, the new kind of human relationships proclaimed in the beatitudes." Arrupe, *Letter and Document on Inculturation*, 244 (n. 23).

55. Ibid., 230.

56. "It is not the church that has a mission of salvation to fulfill in the world; it is the mission of the Son and the Spirit through the Father that includes the church." J. Moltmann, *The Church in the Power of the Spirit: A Contribution to Messianic Ecclesiology* (London: SCM Press, 1977), 64.

57. *Aparecida* 518.

58. The *Aparecida Document* describes the new situation to which the Church must respond as follows: "This should lead us to contemplate the

faces of those who suffer. Among them are the indigenous and Afro-
American communities, which often are not treated with dignity and
equality of conditions; many women who are excluded because of their
sex, race, or socioeconomic situation; young people who receive a poor
education and have no opportunities to advance in their studies or to
enter into the labor market so as to move ahead and establish a family;
many poor people, unemployed, migrants, displaced, landless peasants,
who seek to survive in the informal market; boys and girls subjected to
child prostitution, often linked to sex tourism; also children victims of
abortion. Millions of people and families live in dire poverty and even go
hungry. We are also concerned about those addicted to drugs, differently-
abled people, bearers and victims of serious diseases such as malaria, tu-
berculosis, and HIV-AIDS, who suffer from loneliness and are excluded
from family and community life. Nor do we forget those who are kid-
napped and the victims of violence, terrorism, armed conflicts, and public insecurity; likewise the elderly, who, in addition to feeling excluded
from the production system, often find themselves rejected by their family as people who are a nuisance and useless. Finally, we are pained by the
inhuman situation of the vast majority of prisoners, who also need us to
stand with them and provide fraternal aid. A globalization without solidarity has a negative impact on the poorest groups." *Aparecida* 65.

59. Ibid.

60. Ibid., 550.

61. Cf. *Aparecida* 146.

62. *Aparecida* 399.

63. Pope Paul VI, Apostolic Pilgrimage to Bogotá, homily during
the Mass for Colombian peasants, Bogotá, August 23, 1968.

64. *Aparecida* 366.

65. Ibid., 368.

66. Ibid., 370.

67. Ibid., 366.

68. The then cardinal Bergoglio warned of these dangers subse-
quently in his homily on April 7, 2008: "This reduction of the of the entire realm of our human world (cf. Acts 1:6), this wish to domesticate the
Lord... the temptation to idolatry may also take place in the attempt to
reduce ministry to mere gesture or the temptation of superficiality offered
to us by the "*prêt à porter*" refuge of gnostic theologies or spiritualities...;
and also the temptation of claiming or seeking... a self-referential Church,
which ultimately cannot go out of itself toward proclamation, and in its
cloistered psychology, loses joy." J. M. Bergoglio, Homily, Buenos Aires,
April 7, 2008.

69. Cf. *Aparecida* 226.

70. The expression "popular mystique" was coined by Jorge Seibold, SJ, and then introduced into the Aparecida document. Cf. J. Seibold, *La mística popular* (Mexico City: Buena Prensa, 2006).

71. *Aparecida* 259.

72. *Aparecida* 263.

73. *Aparecida* 259.

74. S. Rubin and F. Ambrogetti, *El Jesuita: Conversaciones con el Cardenal Jorge Bergoglio, SJ* (Buenos Aires: Ediciones B, 2010), 88.

75. Ibid., 169. Over the course of the interview, Bergoglio repeatedly insists on the importance of preserving cultures and creating global and ecclesial dialogue on the basis of what is proper to each cultural form without being absorbed or extinguished by external ideological forms, which can range from the political or economic to the religious.

76. Conferencia Episcopal Argentina, *Orientaciones pastorales para el trienio 2012–2014*, n. 28.

77. *Aparecida* 476.

78. C. Galli, "La teología pastoral de Aparecida: una de las raíces latinoamericanas de *Evangelii Gaudium*," *Gregorianum*, 96 (2015): 44.

79. *Aparecida*, 552.

80. Meeting of Pope Francis with the CELAM Committee, Río de Janeiro, 2013.

81. "It is therefore obvious that the solidarity of the human race and Christian brotherhood demand the elimination as far as possible of these discrepancies. With this object in view, people all over the world must co-operate actively with one another in all sorts of ways, so as to facilitate the movement of goods, capital and men from one country to another. We shall have more to say on this point later on." Pope John XXIII, *Mater et Magistra* 155.

82. "Christians should cooperate willingly and wholeheartedly in establishing an international order that includes a genuine respect for all freedoms and amity between all. This is all the more pressing since the greater part of the world is still suffering from so much poverty" (*GS* 88).

83. Pope Paul VI, *Populorum Progressio* 44.

84. "Our social conduct is an integral part of our following of Christ." *Puebla* 476.

85. H. de Lubac, *Christ and the Common Destiny of Man* (San Francisco: Ignatius Press, 1988, original 1947), 15.

86. Cf. O. Rodríguez Maradiaga, "La importancia de la nueva evangelización," *Origins* 43, no. 24 (November 14, 2013): 375.

87. "It is not in soul-searching or constant introspection that we encounter the Lord: self-help courses can be useful in life, but to live our priestly life going from one course to another, from one method to an-

other, leads us to become Pelagians and to minimize the power of grace, which comes alive and flourishes to the extent that we, in faith, go out and give ourselves and the Gospel to others, giving what little ointment we have to those who have nothing, nothing at all." Pope Francis, Homily, Holy Thursday, March 28, 2013.

88. *Evangelii Nuntiandi* 32.

89. "If the developing nations and regions do not attain liberation through development, there is a real danger that the conditions of life created especially by colonial domination may evolve into a new form of colonialism in which the developing nations will be the victims of the interplay of international economic forces." *Second General Assembly of the Synod of Bishops*, 1971.

90. Pope Francis, Apostolic Visit to Paraguay. Address to representatives of Civil Society, July 11, 2015.

91. Pope Francis, Apostolic Visit to Bolivia, July 9, 2015.

92. Cf. Congreso Misionero Latinoamericano CAM 4—Comla 9, Instrumento de participación, 77–78; 83–84.

93. *Puebla* 386.

94. P. Trigo, *Relaciones humanizadoras: Un imaginario alternativo*. (Santiago, Chile: Ediciones Universidad Alberto Hurtado, 2013), 317.

95. Cf. J. M. Bergoglio, *Ponerse la patria al hombro* (Buenos Aires: Claretiana, 2005).

96. "Urban culture is hybrid, dynamic, and changing, because it combines multiple forms, values, and lifestyles, and it affects all groups. Peripheral-urban culture is the result of the huge migrations of generally poor people who settled around cities in peripheries of extreme poverty. In these cultures, the problems of identity and belonging, relationship, living space and home are increasingly complex." *Aparecida* 58.

97. Trigo, *Relaciones humanizadoras*, 293–94.

98. Pope Francis, Apostolic Visit to Paraguay.

99. Trigo, *Relaciones humanizadoras*, 292.

100. A. Methol Ferré, *De Río a Puebla. Etapas históricas de la Iglesia en América Latina (1945–1980)* (Bogotá: CELAM, 1980), 5.

101. "The Church is not of any culture, but it cannot live without appropriating from cultures; hence it bears in itself the inheritance of various cultures, and this is so even though the Church transcends any culture, it inevitably integrates the concrete historic being of the Church itself. The Church transcends cultures, but it is not only in them, but it 'drags' them in its memory, its being, and it must 'get rid of,' 'be purified' of some cultures in order to penetrate into others. The Church is an identity in constant cultural metamorphoses." A. Methol Ferré, "Visión histórica de los cristianos ante la cultura. En la

Modernidad: Iglesia y cultura," in *Teología de la cultura* (Bogotá: CELAM, 1989), 12.

4. Pastoral Geopolitics of Peoples and Their Cultures

1. Pope Francis, *Letter to President Vladimir Putin of the Russian Federation on the occasion of the Meeting of the G20 in Saint Petersburg*, September 4, 2013.

2. "Renewed diplomacy requires new diplomats who are capable of restoring a sense of community to international life by eliminating the logic of individualism, unfair competition and the desire to be first, by promoting an ethic of solidarity, by replacing the ethic of power which has been reduced to a pattern of thinking used to justify force ... This is the key to the rebirth of that unity among peoples that makes differences its own without ignoring the historical, political, religious, biological, psychological and social elements which express their diversity." Cf. *L'Osservatore Romano*, weekly edition in Spanish, year XLV, no. 46 (2339), November 15, 2013. (Pope Francis, Foreword to the book by Cardinal T. Bertone, *La diplomacia pontificia en un mundo globalizado* [Vatican City: Libreria Editrice Vaticana, 2013]).

3. Cf. Pope Francis, *Apostolic Journey to Cuba. Address at José Martí International Airport*, Havana, September 19, 2015.

4. Pope Francis, Address to the Participants in the Plenary Session of the Pontifical Academy of Social Sciences, Saturday, April 18, 2015.

5. Pope Francis, Address to Signers of the *Declaration of Religious Leaders against Slavery*, Casina Pío IV, December 2, 2014.

6. "Neo-liberalism, as it is understood in Latin America, is a radical conception of capitalism that tends to absolutize the market and transform it into the means, the method, and the end of all intelligent and rational human behavior. According to this conception, people's lives, the functioning of societies, and the policy of governments are subordinated to the market. This absolute market disallows regulation in any area. It is unfettered, without any financial, labor, technological, or administrative restrictions. This current of thought and action tends to turn the economic theory of some of the most brilliant economists of modern capitalism, the authors of neoclassic thought, into a total ideology ... Therefore, neo-liberalism is not equivalent to an economy that acknowledges the importance of the market of all goods and services without making it an absolute, nor is it the equivalent of liberal democracy." *Letter and Study Document on Neoliberalism in Latin America of the Jesuit Provincials of Latin America*. Published in *Promotio Iustitiae* 67 (1997).

7. Cf. Ibid.

8. Cf. J. C. Scannone, "La globalization como hecho e ideología," in *Argentina: Alternativas frente a la globalization* (Buenos Aires: San Pablo, 1999), 253–90.

9. Ibid.

10. Pope Francis, *Second World Meeting of Popular Movements*.

11. *Evangelii Gaudium* 55.

12. Pope Francis, *Address during Aonferral of the Charlemagne Prize*, May 6, 2016.

13. A. Methol Ferré, *Los Estados continentales and el Mercosur.* (Buenos Aires: Ediciones del Instituto Superior Dr. Arturo Jauretche, 2009), 90–91.

14. "Various similar peoples make up a culture. Various cultures in encounter, in interpenetration, make up an *ecumene*. The *ecumene* is where various high cultures gather, penetrate, and mutually transform one another. The *ecumene* entails tension of a plurality of different cultures mixing together. Hence the *ecumene* also points toward an unfolding, a new synthesis or catholicity. The *ecumene* is a concrete exigency of new universality, through integration of different cultural bodies, by a new deep synthesis which is able to assume and transfigure the conflictive whole into a new broad unity." A. Methol Ferré, "Pueblo nuevo en la *ecumene*" *Nexo* 5 (1985): 75.

15. In his apostolic journeys, Pope Francis always insists that "leaders of social, cultural and political life have the particular duty to offer all citizens the opportunity to be worthy contributors of their own future, within their families and in all areas where human social interaction takes place." Pope Francis, Apostolic Visit to Mexico. Meeting with Authorities, Representatives of Civil Society, and the Diplomatic Corps, February 13, 2016.

16. Pope Francis, Apostolic Visit to the Central African Republic. Meeting with Authorities and the Diplomatic Corps, November 29, 2015.

17. The text goes on to say: "In the diversity of peoples who experience the gift of God, each in accordance with its own culture, the Church expresses her genuine catholicity and shows forth the beauty of her varied face" (*EG* 116).

18. Pope Francis, Homily, January 1, 2016.

19. "In the face of this negative globalization which is paralyzing, diplomacy is called to undertake a task of reconstruction, rediscovering its prophetic dimension, determining that which we could call the utopia of the good and, if necessary, reclaiming it. It is not a matter of abandoning this healthy realism which is a virtue in each diplomat, not a technique; but

of overcoming the predominance of the contingent, the limit of pragmatic action which often has the flavor of turning inward. A way of thinking and acting, which if it prevails, limits social and political action and hinders the building of the common good." *L'Osservatore Romano*, weekly edition in Spanish, year XLV, no. 46 (2339), November 15, 2013. (Pope Francis, Foreword to the book by Cardinal T. Bertone, *La diplomacia pontificia en un mundo globalizado* [Vatican City: Libreria Editrice Vaticana, 2013]).

20. "The true utopia of the good, which is not ideology or mere philanthropy, through diplomatic action may express and solidify this brother/sisterliness present in the roots of the human family and from there called to grow, to expand to give its fruits." Ibid.

21. Pope Francis, Apostolic Visit to the Central African Republic.

22. E. Przywara, *En torno a una idea de Europa* (Buenos Aires: Instituto Thomas Falkner, SJ, 2015), 91. This work was first published in German in 1955.

23. Ibid.

24. Cf. A. Methol Ferré, "La Iglesia en América Latina," *Nexo* 4 (1986): 43 ff.

25. Pope Pius XII, *Christmas Message*, Published in *Acta Apostolicam Sedis XXVIII* (1946).

26. *La Elevatezza: Discurso sobre la supranacionalidad de la Iglesia*, February 20, 1946, 23.

27. Ibid., no. 6.

28. A. Methol Ferré et al., *Pueblo e Iglesia en América Latina* (Bogota: Paulinas, 1973).

29. Pope Francis, Speech to the Diplomatic corps accredited to the Holy See, March 22, 2013.

30. "Dialogue is for the common good and the common good is sought by starting from our differences, constantly leaving room for new alternatives. In other words, look for something new. When dialogue is authentic, it ends up with—allow me to use the word and to use it in a noble way—a new agreement, in which we all agree on something...Conflict exists: we have to embrace it, we have to try and resolve it as far as possible, but with the intention of achieving that unity which is not uniformity, but rather a unity in diversity. " Pope Francis, Address to Representatives of Civil Society, Paraguay, July 11, 2015.

31. Pope Francis, Apostolic Visit to Mexico. Meeting with Authorities, Civil Society, and the Diplomatic Corps, February 13, 2016.

32. "The question today is for human freedom, for the capacity to be subject, for the dignity and absolute value of each person. The state and the market are institutions that can contribute to the recognition of and respect for human rights. But they are not in a position to ground

them nor to achieve them, because that pertains only to subjects. In this latter dimension, that of subjectivity, the presence of the church is irreplaceable. Not because it is the only instance in which subjectivity is attained, but because it refers subjectivity to an absolute and transcendent truth, which can nevertheless be found and experienced in the communities of witnesses that make up the ecclesial fabric." CELAM. *Teología de la cultura*. (Bogotá: CELAM, 1989), 129.

33. The Jesuit Pedro Trigo explains the two horizons coexisting in the *Aparecida Document*. The first is the one emphasized by Cardinal Bergoglio, "which is that of salvation taking place in history, from which it is clear that the signs of the times must be interpreted. That requires that believers be immersed in ongoing history in order to see where the action of the Spirit is taking place, and to act in accordance with it. If, however, the theological horizon postulates that salvation was carried out by a single person and that one participates in it in worship, although this new life then redounds throughout all of life, history is merely the place to which the fruits of redemption are brought, not the place where it occurs." P. Trigo, "Aparecida: dos horizontes y convergencias de fondo," *SIC* 698 (2007): 359.

34. Pope Francis, Address to the Diplomatic Corps Accredited to the Holy See, January 11, 2016.

35. J. M. Bergoglio, Foreword to G. Carriquiry, *Una apuesta por América Latina* (Buenos Aires: Ed. Suramericana, 2005), 10ff.

36. "The first task is to put the economy at the service of peoples . . . where human beings, in harmony with nature, structure the entire system of production and distribution in such a way that the abilities and needs of each individual find suitable expression in social life." This passage, taken from the pope's address to popular movements in Bolivia on July 9, 2015, was cited during his apostolic journey to Kenya, when he visited the office of the United Nations in Nairobi, on November 27, 2015.

37. "The peoples whom we often admire for their culture are those that cultivate their principles and laws for centuries, those for whom their *ethos* is sacred, even though they have flexibility in dealing with changing times or pressures from other peoples and power centers." J. M. Bergoglio, homily at the May 25 *Te Deum*, Buenos Aires 2005.

38. "Nothing solid and lasting can be obtained unless it is forged through a vast endeavor of education, mobilization, and constructive participation by peoples, in other words, of persons, and families, of the most diverse communities and associations, of an organized community that unleashes the best resources of humanity, which come from our tradition and which bring together the great popular and national convergences

around sets of ideas and strategic goals for the common good." J. M. Bergoglio, Foreword, *Una Apuesta por América Latina*, 9.

39. "Pastoral and political activity alike seek to gather in this polyhedron the best of each. There is a place for the poor and their culture, their aspirations and their potential. Even people who can be considered dubious on account of their errors have something to offer which must not be overlooked" (*EG* 236).

40. "The purpose of evangelization is plainly eschatological: to make the 'new man' a 'new humankind,' and it seeks to anticipate in history, at each phase of history, insofar as possible, something of the final renewal. Through evangelization, that is, through the transformation and renewal that it arouses and insofar as it arouses it, our human history unfolds as sacred history, history of salvation; that is, as somewhat anticipated eschatological renewal." L. Gera, "Puebla: evangelización de la cultura," *Teología* 33 (1979): 88.

41. "Our political and diplomatic language would do well to be inspired by mercy, which never loses hope." Pope Francis, Message for the 50th World Communications Day, January 24, 2016.

42. Pope Francis, Apostolic Journey to Mexico. Homily in Ciudad Juárez, February 17, 2016.

43. A. Spadaro, "La diplomazia di Francesco," *Civiltà Cattolica* 3975 (2016): 212.

44. Pope Francis, Address to Representatives of Civil Society, Paraguay July 11, 2015.

45. Pope Francis, Address to the Second World Meeting of Popular Movements, Bolivia, July 9, 2015.

46. Ibid.

47. Pope Francis, Address to Representatives of Civil Society, Paraguay, July 11, 2015.

48. "The whole is greater than the part, but it is also greater than the sum of its parts. There is no need, then, to be overly obsessed with limited and particular questions. We constantly have to broaden our horizons and see the greater good which will benefit us all. But this has to be done without evasion or uprooting. We need to sink our roots deeper into the fertile soil and history of our native place, which is a gift of God. We can work on a small scale, in our own neighborhood, but with a larger perspective. Nor do people who wholeheartedly enter into the life of a community need to lose their individualism or hide their identity; instead, they receive new impulses to personal growth. The global need not stifle, nor the particular prove barren" (*EG* 235).

49. Interculturality is assumed by Francis based on accompaniment and fostering of processes that favor "the active participation of the great

excluded majorities." As he said at the First World Meeting of Popular Movements: "Such proactive participation overflows the logical procedures of formal democracy...and calls us to create new forms of participation that include popular movements." They are a real sign of "including the excluded in the building of a common destiny." Interculturality takes place in them, as does the interreligious and ecumenical dimension. Cf. Pope Francis, First World Meeting of Popular Movements.

50. Pope Francis, Address to Representatives of Civil Society, Paraguay, July 11, 2015.

51. *Medellín* 9.

52. *Evangelii Gaudium* 198.

53. "Many ask me: 'Father, why do you speak so much about those in need, about excluded people and people who are on the side of the path?' Simply because this is the reality and the response to this reality is in the heart of the gospel. Because the attitude we adopt when faced with this reality is what we will be judged on, as explained in Matthew 25." Pope Francis, Meeting with Civil, Economic and Political Leaders, Quito, July 7, 2015.

54. J. M. Bergoglio, *La nación por construir: Utopía–Pensamiento–Compromiso*. Words of Cardinal Jorge Mario Bergoglio SJ, addressing the Eighth Archdiocesan Workshop on Social Ministry, Buenos Aires, June 25, 2005. http://www.aica.org/aica/documentos_files/Obispos_Argentinos/Bergoglio/2005/2005_06_25_JornadasPastoralSocial.htm.

55. Pope Francis, Apostolic Journey to Cuba. Homily in the Plaza of the Revolution José Martí," Havana, September 20, 2015.

56. J. M. Bergoglio, Address at the Thirteenth Archdiocesan Workshop on Social Ministry, Buenos Aires, October 16, 2010. This workshop was held under the slogan: "Toward a Bicentenary in Justice and Solidarity 2010–2016. We as Citizens, We as People."

57. *Evangelii Gaudium* 220.

58. Bergoglio, *La nación por construir.*

59. "In this light, and in an increasingly interdependent world, we see ever more clearly the need for interreligious understanding, friendship and collaboration in defending the God-given dignity of individuals and peoples, and their right to live in freedom and happiness. By upholding respect for that dignity and those rights, the religions play an essential role in forming consciences, instilling in the young the profound spiritual values of our respective traditions, and training good citizens, capable of infusing civil society with honesty, integrity and a world view which values the human person over power and material gain." Pope Francis, Apostolic Journey to Kenya. Address in the Ecumenical and Interreligious Meeting in the Hall of the Apostolic Nuntiature in Nairobi, November 26, 2015.

60. "But big cities also conceal the faces of all those people who don't appear to belong, or are second-class citizens. In big cities, beneath the roar of traffic, beneath 'the rapid pace of change,' so many faces pass by unnoticed because they have no 'right' to be there, no right to be part of the city. They are the foreigners, the children who go without schooling, those deprived of medical insurance, the homeless, the forgotten elderly. These people stand at the edges of our great avenues, in our streets, in deafening anonymity. They become part of an urban landscape which is more and more taken for granted, in our eyes, and especially in our hearts." Pope Francis, Apostolic Journey to the United States. Homily in Madison Square Garden, New York, September 25, 2015.

5. FROM ECCLESIAL CULTURE TO PERSONAL ENCOUNTER WITH JESUS

1. This was recognized by a young man during the meeting with students from Jesuit schools in Italy and Albania on July 6, 2013: "Father, above all my gratitude and that of all the kids I have heard these days, because finally with you we have found this message of hope which we used to feel obliged to find out in the world. Now being able to hear it in our house is something that for us is very powerful. Especially, Father, if I may say so, this light was lit here where we young people were really beginning to lose hope. And so thank you, because it has really reached the depths."

2. Pope Francis, interview with the editor of *Civiltá Cattolica*, August 19, 2013. Also in *America*, September 30, 2013.

3. Ibid.

4. *Evangelii Gaudium* 115.

5. Pope Francis, Meeting with the CELAM Coordinating Committee, Río de Janeiro, July 28, 2013.

6. Cf. S. Madrigal, *Unas lecciones sobre el Vaticano II y su legado* (Madrid: Universidad Pontificia Comillas, 2012), 424–37.

7. *Gaudium et Spes* 31.

8. *Gaudium et Spes* 40.

9. *Gaudium et Spes* 1.

10. With the understanding that the great human questions about "the meaning of life, activity, and death" (*GS* 41) are the same questions as those of the ecclesial community.

11. *Gaudium et Spes* 3.

12. *Gaudium et Spes* 1.

13. Cf. *Gaudium et Spes* 2.

14. Cf. *Gaudium et Spes* 40. With modest pretensions, the ecclesial community, "goes forward together with humanity and experiences the

same earthly lot which the world does. She serves as a leaven and as a kind of soul for human society as it is to be renewed in Christ and transformed into God's family" (*GS* 40).

15. *Evangelii Gaudium* 120.

16. "We ought to ask ourselves: are we really church united to Christ, in order to go out to proclaim it to everyone, even, and especially, to those whom I call the 'existential peripheries,' or are we closed in on ourselves, in our groups, in our little chapels?" Pope Francis, Address to Participants in the Pilgrimage from the Diocese of Brescia, June 22, 2013.

17. Cf. T. Dietrich, *Die Theologie der Kirche bei Robert Bellarmin.* (Paderborn: Bonifatius, 1999). Bellarmine's work was published in Ingolstadt in three volumes between 1586 and 1593.

18. Cf. Venezuelan Plenary Council, *Evangelization de la cultura en Venezuela*, 62.

19. "And to seek God in all things, in all fields of knowledge, of art, of science, of political, social and economic life, studies, sensibility and experiences are necessary...All this requires keeping the heart and mind open, avoiding the spiritual sickness of self-reference. Even the church, when she becomes self-referencing, gets sick, grows old. May our sight, well fixed on Christ, be prophetic and dynamic toward the future: in this way you will always be young and audacious in your reading of events! Pope Francis, To the community of writers of *Civiltá Cattólica*, June 14, 2013. See also Meeting with the Brazilian Bishops, Río de Janeiro, July 27, 2013; Meeting with the CELAM Coordinating Committee; Address to the Communion and Liberation Movement, March 7, 2015.

20. Pope Francis believes that the this self-referentiality had something to do with the split from the Eastern church, and that it ought to give way, as Pope John Paul II sought, to a better understanding of primacy. See Pope Francis, press conference of the Holy Father during the return flight to Rome, November 30, 2014.

21. "The Church is an institution, but when she makes herself a 'center," she becomes merely functional, and slowly but surely turns into a kind of NGO. The Church then claims to have a light of her own, and she stops being that *mysterium lunae* of which the Church Fathers spoke. She becomes increasingly self-referential and loses her need to be missionary. From an 'institution' she becomes a 'enterprise.' She stops being a bride and ends up being an administrator; from being a servant, she becomes an 'inspector.' Aparecida wanted a Church which is bride, mother and servant, more a facilitator of faith than an inspector of faith." Pope Francis, Meeting with the CELAM Coordinating Committee.

22. "And it calls for sharing with the holy people of God who live on the outskirts of history. Decentralize. In order to live and bear fruit, every charism is asked to decentralize, in order that Jesus Christ alone is at the center." Pope Francis, Address to the Italian Conference of Major Superiors, November 7, 2014.

23. K. Rahner, "Dogmatic Notes on 'Ecclesiological Piety," in *Theological Investigations V: Later Writings* (New York: Crossroads, 1970), 341.

24. Ibid., 350.

25. "The Church is not the first object of faith; belief in her rests on a faith (and its motives of credibility) which does not refer to the Church but to Christ and to God. Since the Church is also attained by means of this latter faith, she is also an object of faith. Hence it cannot be said either in theory or in practice (at least in most cases) that one believes in the Gospel simply because the Church is the object of one's faith. Rather (in spite of what St. Augustine says) the Church is an object of one's faith because one believes the gospel." Ibid., 352.

26. Ibid., 364.

27. Venezuelan Plenary Council, *Evangelization de la cultura en Venezuela*, p. 62.

28. Ibid., no. 70.

29. *Gaudium et Spes* 45.

30. *Evangelii Gaudium* 7.

31. Pope Francis, *Apostolic Letter of his Holiness Pope Francis to All Consecrated People on the Occasion of the Year of Consecrated Life*, November 21, 2014.

32. *Gaudium et Spes* 72.

33. Rahner, "Dogmatic Notes," 357.

34. *Per hunc Spiritum, qui est "pignus hereditatis"* (Eph 1:14); *totus homo interius restauratur, usque ad "redemptionem corporis"* (Rom 8:23); *Gaudium et Spes* 22.

35. *Tamen fraternum hominum colloquium non in istis progressibus, sed profundius in personarum communitate perficitur, quae mutuam reverentiam erga plenam earum dignitatem spiritualem exigit* (GS 23).

36. *Gaudium et Spes* 32.

37. Ibid.

38. Ibid.

39. "The personal entrusting of each other to each other, which is included in the *credere in Deum*, cannot be applied to the Church. However much we may and must 'personify' the Church, however much she may be more than the numerical sum of individual Christians, however much she is a reality which is not a juridical reality or fiction, an ideolog-

ical structure or a 'moral unit'—the Church as such is not a person, i.e., the Church insofar as she must be distinguished from real individual persons, cannot be conscious of herself, cannot justify herself, cannot decide, nor is she eternal." Rahner, "Dogmatic Notes," 549.

40. "In some fashion salvation history has to do with salvation in history; but on the other hand it implies that the salvation proclaimed by the Church in history must be proclaimed by it out of salvation history itself and not out of other things foreign to it." I. Ellacuría, *Conversión de la Iglesia al Reino de Dios* (Santander, 1984), 220.

41. "For we understand the Church when we [see it] as the historically and socially constituted assembly of those who have the courage to believe, who as it were confess to one another the secret enormity of the faith living in the ground of their being, and who—by professing, praying, celebrating and rendering present the very basis of their courage, i.e., the Death and Resurrection of Jesus—give one courage to make this daring absolute claim to infinite grace. Thus faith comes through the Church and the Church through faith." Rahner, "Dogmatic Notes," 345.

42. Ibid., 351.

43. Vatican I had already spoken of the Church as "*motivum credibilitatis*" (in itself and by itself), and as "*divinae suae legationis testimonium irrefragabile*" (to others and to God) (*DH* 3013). But it was after Vatican II that the way of witness was adopted as constitutive dimension of the Church's being.

44. Among those who have developed this argument is Walter Kasper, in his work *Das Absolute in der Geschichte* (Mainz 1965).

45. *Gaudium et Spes* 3.

46. R. Tello, "Evangelization y cultura," in in *Pueblo y cultura popular* (Buenos Aires: Patria Grande-Ágape, 2014), 227. (These words are also found in his personal notes, 1996).

47. L. Gera, "La fe en un mundo en crisis," in *Escritos teológico-pastorales de Lucio Gera. I: Del preconcilio a la Conferencia de Puebla (1956–1981)*, ed. V. Azcuy, C. Galli, and M. González (Buenos Aires: Ágape, 2006), 863.

48. The three aspects are explained in Gera's "La fe en un mundo en crisis."

49. Gera, "La fe en un mundo en crisis," 864.

50. "Today very many ecclesial institutions (even legal institutions), maintain customs and values, but they cannot be said to be culturally dominant in the doctrine of Christian life that the Church transmits to the world." R. Tello, "Evangelization y cultura," 232.

51. Cf. J. Ratzinger, *Relativism: The Central Problem for Faith Today:* Conference at the meeting of the Congregation for the Doctrine of the

Faith with the presidents of the Doctrinal Commissions of the Bishops' Conferences of Latin America, held in Guadalajara, Mexico, in May 1996.

52. The three aspects are explained in L. Gera, "La fe en un mundo en crisis," 865.

53. Cf. R. Tello, "Evangelization y cultura," 234–36.

54. Ibid., 245.

55. Ibid.

56. "In the sense that that the founding events of an objective redemption—Christ died for us once and for all—keep happening, not in the sense that there occur new public revelations, the cycle of which closed in the apostolic period." L. Gera, "Teología de los procesos históricos," 874–75.

57. Ibid.

58. Pope Francis, Address to the Curia, December 22, 2014.

59. Cf. *Joint International Commission for the Theological Dialogue between the Roman Catholic Church and the Orthodox Church: The Ecclesiological and Canonical Consequences of the Sacramental Nature of the Church. Ecclesial communion, Conciliarity and Authority.* Ravenna, October 13, 2007, no. 7.

60. Pope Francis, Homily, February 2, 2015.

61. "Interview given by Pope Francis to Father Antonio Spadaro," *L'Osservatore Romano*, weekly edition in Spanish, year XLV, no. 39 (2333), September 27, 2013.

62. Pope Francis, Address to the Roman Curia.

63. J. M. Bergoglio, *La nación por construir*. Seventh Conference on Social Ministry, June 25, 2005.

Conclusion

1. "How many of us followers of Christ run the risk of losing our ability to be astonished, even with the Lord? That wonder we had on the first encounter seems to diminish, and it can happen to anyone. Indeed it happened to the first pope: 'To whom shall we go Lord? You have the words of eternal life.' And then they betray him, they deny him, the wonder fades away. It happens when we get accustomed to things. The heart is blinded. A heart used to passing by without letting itself be touched; a life which passes from one thing to the next, without ever sinking roots in the lives of the people around us, simply because it is part of the elite who follow the Lord." Pope Francis, Apostolic Visit to Bolivia. Address in the Meeting with Clergy, Religious, and Seminarians at the Coliseum of Colegio Don Bosco, Santa Cruz, July 9, 2015.

2. *Aparecida* 370.

3. "The truth is that only in the mystery of the incarnate Word does the mystery of man take on light. For Adam, the first man, was a figure of Him Who was to come, namely Christ the Lord. Christ, the final Adam, by the revelation of the mystery of the Father and His love, fully reveals humanity to itself and makes its supreme calling clear. It is not surprising, then, that in Him all the aforementioned truths find their root and attain their crown... For by his incarnation the Son of God has united himself in some fashion with every person. He worked with human hands, he thought with a human mind, acted by human choice and loved with a human heart. Born of the Virgin Mary, he has truly been made one of us, like us in all things except sin" (*GS* 22).

4. "The last thing I would tell you—before telling you a few other things too!—is that when we let ourselves be chosen by Jesus, it is to serve: to serve the people of God, to serve the poor, men and women who are outcasts, living on the fringes of society, to serve children and the elderly. But also to serve people who are unaware of their own pride and sin, to serve Jesus in them. Letting ourselves be chosen by Jesus means letting ourselves be chosen to serve, and not to be served." Pope Francis, Apostolic Visit to Nairobi. Address to Clergy, Male and Female religious, and Seminarians at the athletic field of St. Mary's School, November 26, 2015.

5. Pope Francis, Apostolic Visit to Ecuador. Homily at Mass in Bicentenary Park, July 7, 2015.

6. Pope Francis, Apostolic Visit to Paraguay. Address to Representatives of Civil Society at the León Condou Stadium, July 11, 2015.

INDEX